Cure for the Procrastination Puzzle

Blueprint to Develop Atomic Long-Term Habits for Productivity and Get things Done - Learn Why You Do It and Master Your Time with Over 7 Highly Effective Methods

Stephen Patterson

© Copyright 2019 - All rights reserved.

The content contained within this book may not be reproduced, duplicated or transmitted without direct written permission from the author or the publisher.

Under no circumstances will any blame or legal responsibility be held against the publisher, or author, for any damages, reparation, or monetary loss due to the information contained within this book. Either directly or indirectly.

Legal Notice:
This book is copyright protected. This book is only for personal use. You cannot amend, distribute, sell, use, quote or paraphrase any part, or the content within this book, without the consent of the author or publisher.

Disclaimer Notice:

Please note the information contained within this document is for educational and entertainment purposes only. All effort has been executed to present accurate, up to date, and reliable, complete information. No warranties of any kind are declared or implied. Readers acknowledge that the author is not engaging in the rendering of legal, financial, medical or professional advice. The content within this book has been derived from various sources. Please consult a licensed professional before attempting any techniques outlined in this book.

By reading this document, the reader agrees that under no circumstances is the author responsible for any losses, direct or indirect, which are incurred as a result of the use of information contained within this document, including, but not limited to, — errors, omissions, or inaccuracies.

Contents

Chapter 1:
What is Procrastination _____ 1

Chapter 2:
The Life Impact of Procrastination _____ 9

Chapter 3:
Reasons We Procrastinate _____ 17

Chapter 4:
What Can Happen with Productivity _____ 33

Chapter 5:
The Importance of Motivation _____ 41

Chapter 6:
The Impact of Willpower and Self-Discipline _____ 51

Chapter 7:
Overcoming Procrastination _____ 59

Chapter 8:
Figure Out the Reason for Your Procrastination _____ 63

Chapter 9:
Audit Your Goals Weekly _____ 67

Chapter 10:
Get Rid of Negative Self-Talk _____ 75

Chapter 11:
Focus on a Single Task _____ 79

Chapter 12:
Time Chunking _____ 87

Chapter 13:
Reduce Environmental Distractions _____ 95

Chapter 14:
Avoid Being Bored _____ 105

Chapter 15:
Find an Accountability Partner _____ 111

Chapter 16:
Leverage Your Peak-Energy _____ 115

Chapter 17:
Parkinson's Law _____ 123

Chapter 18:
Prioritize Tasks _____ 129

Chapter 19:
Reward Yourself _____ 135

Chapter 20:
FAQs _____ 141

Conclusion: _____ 145

CURE FOR THE PROCRASTINATION PUZZLE

Blueprint to Develop Atomic Long Term Habits for Productivity and Get things Done - Learn Why You Do It and Master Your Time with Over 7 Highly Effective Methods

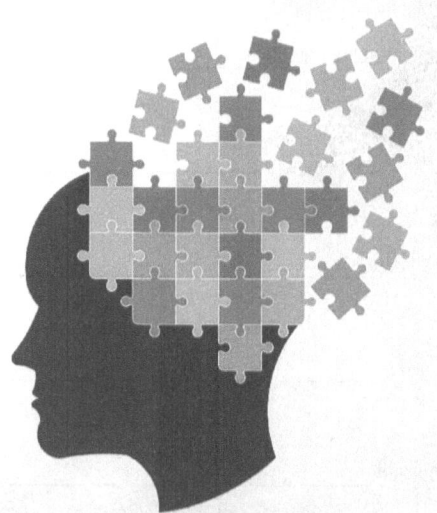

Stephen Patterson

Chapter 1:
What is Procrastination

What exactly does procrastination mean? Pro-crustiness is a Latin word that means "belonging to tomorrow." Procrastination means "putting things off intentionally or habitually." But defining procrastination isn't that simple.

If you have ever found yourself persuading yourself to do things other than those that you should do, you have been the victim of procrastination. Most of the time, you will find yourself performing trivial tasks instead of working on important tasks.

Since the beginning of humanity, people have had to suffer from procrastination. Hesiod, the classic Greek poet, even commented on the issue in his poem *Works and Days*:

- "Do not postpone for tomorrow
- Or the day after tomorrow

- Barns are not filled by those who postpone
- And waste time in aimlessness.
- Work prospers with care;
- He who postpones wrestles with ruin."

The Roman philosopher, Seneca, even warned: "While we waste our time hesitating and postponing, life is slipping away." This quote is the main reason why it is so important that we learn how to overcome procrastination.

Procrastination is probably the main thing blocking you from living your life to its fullest. Some studies have discovered that people will often regret the things that they aren't able to accomplish than the things that they were able to do. Feelings of guilt and regret caused by missed chances will often stay with a person much longer. When a person procrastinates, they waste valuable time that could be used to do something important and meaningful. If you are able to overcome this enemy, you will notice that you can accomplish more and utilize the potential of life.

The True Definition

Cure for the Procrastination Puzzle

Dr. Samuel Johnson, the author of the first comprehensive English dictionary, defined procrastination as "delay" and many still maintain that definition. The Free Dictionary defines procrastination as "slowness as a consequence of not getting around to it."

However, if all that procrastination means is to delay, then we ought to find with placing it alongside concepts like prioritizing and scheduling, but we don't. Take these two examples:

Imagine yourself as a surgeon and you are getting ready to put your patient under general anesthetic. If you discover that they just ate a large meal at a buffet, you have to hold off the operation. The reason for this is that the unconscious patient could empty the contents of their stomachs into their lungs. This would cause digestive juices to dissolve things other than the food.

Now, picture that you are in the Bahamas and have some sport-fishing planned when a category five hurricane blows in. It has winds in excess of 155 miles an hour and waves that crash in at over ten stories high. You push your plans back for fishing by a couple of days.

Both of these stories use delay, but would either of these delays that drowning or dissolving be considered as dilly-dallying? Probably not. Maybe procrastination, perhaps, could mean something more.

Timothy Picryl, a procrastination researcher, explains that "all procrastination is a delay, but not all delay is procrastination." Procrastination is a specific type of delay. Unlike these types of delays, procrastination doesn't have any rationale behind it. This extremely important distinction can be seen more often now. The American Heritage Dictionary defines it as "To put off doing something, especially out of habitual carelessness or laziness."

But the Oxford English Dictionary is the one that gets the closest to the heart of the word. Their definition of procrastination is, "often with the sense of deferring through indecision, when early action would have been preferable."

That brings us to questions of, can procrastination be good? If it's by accident that you choose to delay something purposefully because you believe it would be a good thing to do, then you are not procrastinating. This means you are prioritizing or scheduling, sometimes just so that you can get that thrill of doing something at the last moment. Procrastination is when you end up feeling as if the project should have been finished earlier, but you delayed it anyway. Basically, it means you put something off even though you expect the worse.

Cure for the Procrastination Puzzle

The thing is, the world doesn't always work out the way we want it to, and sometimes luck will be on our side and we discover that what we have been putting off didn't have to be done after all. The way we believe the world is and the way it actually has to be at odds. Otherwise, you get lucky from time to time by procrastinating. Like if you were in Vegas playing roulette. Once in a while, you will pick the right number, but most of the time it's going to land on red.

Still, the majority of people misuse procrastination to describe useful delays, when you could use many different words to describe that problem. People will misuse a lot of other words such as "irony." Whether you want to use the word procrastination correctly or not is up to you, but I will leave you with this thought.

If, on Christmas Eve, you hear the glugging of milk and the munching of cookies coming from your living room, and after some investigation, discover a jolly and chubby old elf that has spent the last 365 days waiting to deliver colorful presents, thank him for his timeliness. He might have been able to come earlier, but you should not define his choice to delay the Yuletide cheer as procrastination.

Today's Decision Paralysis

Now that we've gotten the real definition out of the way, let's look at how it plays out in today's world. Since the world plays into procrastination's hands, learning how to overcome it is an important skill. Over the past 100 years, the average lifespan of humans has doubled. Infant mortality has become a tenth of what it was back then. Each morning, we get up in a world that has less military conflict and less violence than any other area of our history. Most importantly, thanks to the internet, almost all information is just a few clicks away.

There are very few limits on travel. You can go almost anywhere in the world at any time. Speaking another language allows people to communicate efficiently in foreign countries. That phone you have in your pocket comes with more power than the supercomputers from 20 years ago.

There are a staggering number of opportunities in the world. Modern society believes that the freer people are, the happier they will become. If that's the case, why aren't people a lot happier now than they were in the past? With all of the extra freedom to make out own decisions and perform the things we want to, we have now become confused with what should get priority, what is crucial and what isn't, and what is right and wrong. This makes us all more demotivated.

It's important that we set our personal vision and values straight and to establish good habits. This is what can help us to work through procrastination and all of the obstacles that come along with life.

Stephen Patterson

Chapter 2:
The Life Impact of Procrastination

If you were to ask a group of people to raise their hands if they view themselves as a procrastinator, a lot of hands would end up going up. While there are many people that seem to be fine with being a procrastinator, others who admit they procrastinate feel ashamed to admit it. This is normal because, in our culture, procrastination is often seen as a bad word. In America, we tend to celebrate those that are able to put their nose-to-the-grindstone. Procrastination doesn't deserve a place in our economy or culture, but is it really that bad?

There is a fine line between being pressure prompted and procrastinating. Pressure prompted means that you do your best work when you have a deadline looming over your head. While you may have to procrastinate a bit to be pressure prompted, it is procrastination within safe limits. Basically, it's a condition set that is going to provide you just enough pressure to ensure that you stay at the top of your game without creating a lot of chaos, or more importantly, not affecting your team by keeping them from being able to perform their best within the given timeframe.

But what about those who aren't only pressure prompted but real procrastinators? To clear up what I mean, I'm not talking about a person that waits to write their keynote address a couple of days before they are supposed to walk on stage, but rather the person who scribbles out a couple of notes 20 minutes before their speech. If you see this person when you look in the mirror, it is time to start thinking about how this impacts your life if it is left unmanaged.

Procrastination is a problem that impacts a person's physical and mental health, as well as their performance in the workplace and at school. A study published in Psychology Bulletin in 2007, Piers Steel, a psychologist, defined procrastination as "a self-regulatory failure leading to poor performance and reduced wellbeing." He further explained that procrastination is extremely common. Around 80 to 90 percent of college students suffer from procrastination and is something that 95% of people wants to overcome. Steel believes that procrastination is on the rise because people want to receive immediate gratification that they can get through the use of information technology and social media.

While more responsibilities and age do help the majority of people keep their procrastination in check, for some, procrastination isn't an occasional or temporary problem but something that controls their lives and limits their potential.

How bad can procrastination be? Below, I will look at a few of the negative impacts that it can have on your financial, mental, and physical wellbeing.

Mental Health:

In 2010, a study called "I'll Go to Therapy, Eventually," discovered that stress and procrastination had a connection. The study discovered that a lot of procrastination was connected to poor mental health and fewer behaviors to help mental health such as taking time to relax.

Physical Health:

As well as the well-documented link between mental health and procrastination, there is an increasing amount of proof that procrastination can impact a person's physical health. Fuchsia M. Sirois, in a 2003 study, discovered that procrastination was "related to poorer health, treatment delay, perceived stress, and fewer wellness behaviors." While procrastination can affect a lot of health problems, Sirois and team discovered that there were some that were more impacted than others. In a study done in 2015, she concluded that procrastination is one of the many factors that can lead to cardiovascular disease and hypertension, and further concluded that the "maladaptive coping" that is associated with procrastination exasperates the symptoms that are associated with HT/CVD.

Workplace Satisfaction, Performance, And Success

Given how negatively procrastination impacts a person's physical and mental health, it's not surprising that it would also negatively impact a person's workplace performance. Procrastinators will often earn less, spend less time at a job, and hold jobs that have lower intrinsic value. A study performed in 2016 discovered that procrastination tends to be more common for people who are unemployed, which could mean that procrastination could cause unemployment. However, procrastination isn't something that could increase a person's likelihood of leaving a job or not having one. There is at least one other study that found that "job-lock," which means not being able to freely leave a job even if you are unhappy and there is no room for growth, could also be caused by procrastination. On a similar note, procrastination could also cause bad financial decisions.

If you're still not convinced of the detrimental effects that procrastination can have on your life, the following seven effects of procrastination are more specific and relatable.

1. Loss of Precious Time

How much time have you lost from procrastinating? It's not easy to figure, but I'm sure you can come up with an estimate. The worst part of procrastinating is when you realize that you are two, six, or 12 years older and nothing in your life has changed. Where did the time go?

This is a horrible feeling because you can't do anything to get that time back. All you can do is live with the helpless feeling of regret. There is nothing worse than having to feel frustrated with yourself and knowing that you could have made the situation better. All you had to do was take the first step.

2. Opportunities Are Blown

How many opportunities have you missed out on because you didn't jump on it when you have the chance? These are moments where you really kick yourself. What you don't see is that the opportunity could have ended up being life-changing, but you missed out.

The majority of opportunities will only come around once. There are no guaranteed second chances. Opportunities are how the world gives you more, so do yourself a favor and grab hold.

3. Goals Aren't Met

Procrastination will often come in full force when we start to entertain the thoughts of goals, of wanting to change or achieve something new. You could have an extremely strong desire to change, but you aren't able to take those first steps towards it. This is often perplexing and confusing. You will often think to yourself, "Why is it hard to go after something that I want?" Only you know the answer.

You are going to have to explore things a little deeper. People set goals because they want to better their lives in one way or another. If this doesn't happen because of procrastination, you will destroy your odds of bettering your life.

Figure out the root cause of your procrastination if it is keeping you from reaching your goals, otherwise, you won't attain them.

4. Ruined Careers

The way you work has a direct effect on your results, how well you perform, and how much you achieve. Procrastination could be preventing you from reaching deadlines or achieving your monthly goals. What kind of consequence is this going to have on your career?

You could be overlooked for a promotion or you could end up losing your job. You can do your best to hide things for a while, but long-term procrastination at work will end up ruining your career.

5. Low Self-Esteem
This is a common vicious cycle that people will find their self in. We often procrastinate because we have low self-esteem, but procrastinating doesn't just reinforce this feeling, it makes it stronger.

You will begin to question and doubt yourself. You will often start asking yourself, "Why can't I just do it?" Low self-esteem will destroy lives in several different ways. Low self-esteem will cause you to hold yourself back, you feel less than, and it can lead to self-sabotaging acts. Procrastination will slowly destroy your confidence.

6. Poor Decisions
When you make decisions from a procrastination standpoint, they will almost always be poor decisions because of where your mind is. When procrastinating, you will make decisions based on criteria that

wouldn't be there otherwise such as pressure to finally make a decision.

Emotions play a big part in decisions and procrastination plays a big part in how you feel. Poor decision making will have a lot of negative effects on your life, happiness, and results.

7. Damaged Reputation

When you are constantly saying that you are going to do something and then you don't, your reputation is going to become tarnished. Nobody is interested in empty promises.

Besides hurting your reputation, you will damage your self-confidence and self-esteem. You will also find that procrastination will become easier every time because you will no longer feel surprised. People may end up not depending on you anymore and will hold back opportunities because they may worry that you will procrastinate and they will have to clean up your mess.

These are only a few ways your life is affected by procrastination. Procrastination works like any other habit and it can be hard to kick, but it will also make you or break you.

Chapter 3:
Reasons We Procrastinate

Procrastination is one of the sure-fire ways to avoid success in life. Procrastinators are self-sabotaging people and they place obstacles in their own way. They will actually pick paths that harm their performance. Why would a person do something like that?

20% of people identify themselves as a procrastinator. For these people, procrastination is their life and it affects all domains of their life. Their bills aren't paid on time. They miss out on concert tickets. They don't ever cash gift certificates or checks. Their taxes are done late. They will even put off their Christmas shopping until the day before.

It's not a trivial matter, but as a culture, we don't take it seriously. It's seen as a self-regulation problem. There may be more of it in the US than anywhere else because we tend to be nice and not call people out on their "excuses." Let's take a look at the main reasons people procrastinate.

Better Options

A lot of people will have "Too many interests to choose just one!" That fact resonates with the majority of procrastinators. Society expects us to choose one thing and stick with it. Take Mozart for example. He started his career in music at three years old and never allowed anything to interfere, even his deafness.

But what if a person is more of a Leonardo de Vinci, Benjamin Franklin, or Maya Angelo? Where would the world be if these people that they couldn't put off finishing something until tomorrow when something new and exciting presented itself? They were all likely label procrastinators but they turned out okay. That doesn't mean all procrastination is a good thing.

When it detrimentally affects a person's life, then something needs to be done about it. The point is, people will often procrastinate because of the other things that they would rather do. Who wouldn't rather go to a concert than write a boring report for work? Still, that doesn't mean you should.

Lack of Focus

A lack of focus in your life is another common reason a person will procrastinate. A famous idiom says "the person who does not know where they are going always travels further," but for people who are predisposed to procrastinate, this doesn't mesh all that well with them.

If you notice that you often feel directionless or that you don't have a purpose in life, then you likely have a lack of focus. If you haven't created any goals, then it's almost guaranteed that you will lack focus because you don't have a target to work towards. You could feel as if you are drifting your way through your life.

Having a lack of focus will cause procrastination because it prevents you from finding your endpoint. Instead, you will end up using all of your energy in the here and now and you won't have anything to guide you toward productivity.

A lot of younger people will suffer from a lack of focus. They haven't figured out how to set any strong targets or goals, so they will fritter away most of their day. But through effective goal setting, they can overcome this procrastination and will be able to achieve more in their life.

Setting goals for everything you do is a good idea. You can set goals for business, your finances, your career, and anything you can dream you can set a goal for. Having a good goal will encourage you to take some form of action because you won't want to disappoint yourself.

Negative Talk

The things that people will often procrastinate on are the tasks that tend to be more difficult, or they are the tasks that you view to be more difficult. If you often blame yourself when a problem comes up, then you probably don't feel like you are able to ask for help and work through those problems.

This is only going to make your problem worse. You will often tell yourself that you can't do something or that you will mess it up. This will reinforce your procrastination because you now don't have the confidence to do anything. This is a common reason for a person to procrastinate. They lack confidence in their ability to do the job successfully. They are, in fact, more than capable of being able to do it.

This often stems from perfectionism which we will talk about later. Society can sometimes make you feel as if you have to do a perfect job at every little thing you do. That means that you won't start until you feel certain that you will be able to do it perfectly. But this is the absolute worst thing that you can do.

When you take some sort of action, you will achieve an outcome. The outcome could end up being what you are looking for or it may not be. Either way, you will learn something from it and then you can make some improvements or adjustments. If you don't take any sort of action, you won't learn anything.

Don't Know Where to Start
What if the task ends up being too difficult, complex, or unique? What if there are a lot of moving parts that makes it unclear as to where to start? This type of uncertainty is likely to keep you from wanting to start because you don't know what your first step should be.

Even if you have figured out what your first step should be, once you start looking at the whole process, you start to realize that you may have underestimated how much commitment and time it is going to take to finish the task.

How do you overcome this problem? One of the best ways is to use the "getting things done" approach. This is going to help you to break the tasks down into smaller tasks.

No Motivation

Have you ever had the thought that life has gotten in your way, and you haven't been able to accomplish the things you were supposed to? This lack of motivation can end up coming from many different causes, which includes:

- Unclear goals
- Working in a bad environment
- Lack of confidence
- You are around a lot of negativity
- You've not been successful in the past
- Can't find new ideas
- Unexpected emergency
- Other priorities
- Stress
- Fatigue
- Lack of energy

Carnegie Melon University performed a study that found people lack motivation when they can't find value in the possible outcome of their work. But, if people can see how their work is going to connect to their concerns, interests, and goals, they are more likely to like their work and become motivated to invest their energy and time.

The National Academies of Sciences, Engineering, and Medicine published a study that said motivation was made up of two things — goal choice and self-confidence. Self-confidence doesn't give a person motivation on its own but gives a person a judgment about their capabilities for accomplishing their goal

Low Energy
Another common reason for procrastination is low energy levels. If you lack energy, then it's probably a good guess that you won't feel like doing all that much.

This is a common problem for people who have an unhealthy lifestyle. Whether you don't get enough sleep or you eat foods that cause you to feel tired and sluggish, lifestyle facts are able to play a very big part into how inclined you are to get up and do something.

It should be fairly easy to find the problem area in your life. If you are interested in being productive and active, but you lack the actual physical energy to do something, then you probably have a problem with low energy levels.

The cure for this is to try to develop healthier lifestyles. Try to experiment with your exercise, sleep, and diet to figure out the balance that will work for you. There is a whole host of useful info that you can find online to make positive changes in your life, and you probably already have a good idea of the changes that you need to make.

If you aren't able to raise those energy levels, then you may want to speak with your healthcare provider to rule out any underlying cause of your low energy.

Feel Overwhelmed

When you take your first look at a difficult job or a big project, it can become overwhelming to notice how much work you are going to have to do. This doesn't get helped by the fact that you will automatically assume that you will have to do everything by yourself, and you also don't take into account the amount of time that you have to get the job done.

To make sure that you don't get overwhelmed, you will want to break your job down into smaller tasks. This is going to be a common thing that you notice throughout this book. Breaking a project down into smaller parts will help a lot with procrastination.

It's important to remember when you feel overwhelmed, that you can only do so much in one day. Unless you have already delayed the project so much that you have to do it all in one day, you shouldn't be faced with that problem.

Perfectionism

Maybe you are afraid that you are going to make a mistake in your project and then expose a weakness to those around you. The fear of making a mistake is a very real thing and it can be so bad that people will put off some of their most important projects because of it.

Carol Dweck, Ph.D., a Stanford University psychologist, talks about the power of a person's mindset. She relates a person's success in the arts, work, sports, school, and other parts of the human endeavor to the way a person thinks about their abilities and talents.

She explains that people will either have a growth mindset or a fixed mindset. Those that have a fixed mindset think that the abilities they have can't get any better, so they focus on their current talents or intelligence and believe that they can't develop them.

They honestly believe that they were born with what they have and that there isn't anything they can do to make it better. These people will also believe that they don't need effort for success if they have talent. They think that the talent is natural.

A fixed mindset can be very dangerous because it hinders a person's ability to make positive changes, grow, and learn.

Alternatively, a growth mindset will let a person believe that their abilities are able to prosper and can be developed through hard work and dedication. They believe that a person's talents and brains are just a starting point. They are born with their strengths, but they don't have a limit on what they can do. The growth mindset helps to create a desire to learn and gives them the ability to overcome their problems to be successful.

Dweck also explained that a person's mindset can reveal how great managers, teachers, and parents can advance within their careers and achieve amazing things. When you have the right mindset, a person can motivate, teach, and lead in a way that is able to positively change the lives of others.

Hillary Rettig believes that people who procrastinate because of perfectionism will often have a fixed mindset. This means that they will avoid doing things because they are worried that they will make a mistake and look less than perfect. They expect their work to be perfect. Since they have the belief that they will fail if the task doesn't line up with their talents, it is best to avoid until it has to be done.

While some people believe that being a perfectionist is a good thing, it actually ends up being detrimental. It comes with a very dangerous mix of anti-productive attitudes and habits that discourage progress. Although it is often confused with having high standards, perfectionism limits success to something that is unrealistic. This is a standard that won't ever be achieved, so why even try?

Fear of Success

Everybody is pretty familiar with a fear of failure, but there is another side to that coin and that's a fear of success. This is when a person procrastinates because they are afraid of the consequences of their achievements. They may fear that they will do a good job, and then next time, more will be expected from them. It could be succeeding puts them in the limelight, but they prefer to be in the background.

This type of procrastination may indicate that there is an internal identity conflict. If your achievement and self-worth are connected, then you may find that you question yourself about how much you have to do in order to be "good enough." Every success will only set you up for another, bigger challenge.

If your family acceptance and self-worth are connected, then how much more will you have to do to make them satisfied? Every success will open a door to higher expectations.

This will often lead to feelings of identity loss and you may not be able to claim your successes as your own. Procrastination or inaction may be the way that you cope with all of the pressures you are placing on yourself by trying to be "good enough."

Fear of Failure or The Unknown
Imagine this, you wake up one morning and notice a new mole has appeared on your arm. You start to feel anxious about the fact that it could be cancer, so you avoid having it checked and hope that it will go away. Does this sound like something you would do? Sometimes people are afraid to do something because they are afraid that it is going to reveal something they don't want.

As it turns out, "What you don't know can't hurt you," isn't all that true. In nearly every single case, if you try to ignore something for too long because you hope it will go away, it is only going to get worse.

University of Michigan researchers performed a study on the effects of letting misinformation stay in a person's mind. The study found that misinformation can stay in a person's memory and continue to influence the way they think, even if they know that they were mistaken. They are also more likely to use the misinformation, especially if it fits into their existing beliefs and create a logical story. This will then cause them to spread the misinformation to others.

This study can be applied to politics, the environment, and to individuals. When you have preconceived notions or misinformation about health issues like, "cancer doesn't run in my family, so it's probably okay," or "the mole is going to go away with some time," can end up doing a lot of damage. The researchers also discovered that a person's personal views and beliefs could end up being big obstacles for changing the believed misinformation. Additionally, attempting to provide them with an unwanted truth that goes against what they had believed can backfire and increase their incorrect ideas. When it comes to personal health problems, ignoring issues instead of facing them head-on can definitely lead to severe problems or death.

Really think about this. What if that mole was cancer that could be easily treated during the early stages, but can end up becoming malignant if it's ignored? If you are proactive in getting it checked out, it would be a simple fix. Or you could decide to procrastinate because you think that everything is going to be fine. This is when what you don't know can hurt you, and your beliefs that it is going to go away on its own will end up being detrimental.

Some other good examples of this problem include not going to the dentist and continuing to believe that the cavity you think you have is going to be okay. Maybe you aren't interested in doing your taxes because until you are faced with the fact that you will have to pay, you don't have to think about it. Maybe you are avoiding a conversation with your significant other to delay the argument that it could create. Every single one of these causes for procrastination is common.

All of this connects back to what the researchers at the University of Michigan found out because in all of these cases the person is not interested in learning the truth. They feel more at ease with the possibility that all will be okay. Ignorance is bliss, so we procrastinate in order to stay happy and ignorant. However, when you ignore these problems, it can lead to grave circumstances.

Cure for the Procrastination Puzzle

Knowledge is power. Even if it turns out to be negative, you didn't get the promotion, the mole is cancer and you own the government money, you will have more opportunities to overcome an even worse situation. Knowing this information is only half of it. After that, you will have to do something to correct it if needed. The next time you think about procrastinating, ask yourself these questions:

- Am I really scared, or have I been told something scary?
- Am I looking to protect myself from a specific outcome?
- Will I be able to handle the outcome?
- Am I afraid of the result or the process?
- Am I trying to convince myself of things that aren't true?
- How often do people die from having to do this?
- What am I going to gain in the long run if I keep putting this off?
- Why am I putting this off?
- What can happen if I continue to ignore the problem?
- What is the worst thing that could happen?

Stephen Patterson

- What is it that I am afraid of?

Chapter 4:
What Can Happen with Productivity

Americans enjoy work. They like to do it. It's actually very common for business professionals to work more than 50 hours a week. Some information suggests that the US is one of a few countries that don't have a requirement for time off for employees.

Some cities work their employees more than others. Columbia, Missouri received the title of the hardest working city by Forbes, which was followed by Hartford, Connecticut, and then Norfolk, Virginia.

But does being productive mean, you have to be a workaholic? Why is that Americans are so obsessed about being productive and what types of factors encourage this behavior?

When you look at productivity from a business definition, it is defined as, "a measure of the efficiency of a person, machine, factory, or system in converting inputs into useful outputs." By that definition, American workers have increased their productivity for the past few years. However, wages which these workers directly connect with the productivity have stayed the same.

Studies and experts have discovered that productivity in humans is impacted by psychological factors. And the answer is bigger than looking at pictures of cuddly little animals.

The way the brain functions plays a big role in why and how people are productive or not so productive. Several different experiments that were performed at a factory just outside of Chicago, between the years of 1924 and 1932, which was later called the Hawthorne Effect, found that the productivity of the workers was increased because of psychological stimulus that made them feel important or singled out.

According to David M. Reiss, MD, this study makes sense for the fact that the average person, because whether unconsciously or consciously will feel insecure and have some form of vulnerabilities of self-esteem, so any intervention that is able to reduce those insecurities and help their self-esteem will make the mood better, improve productivity, reduce anxiety, and improve their motivation.

If the person is singled out in such a way that makes it feel parental, people that tend to be dependent will often respond in a positive manner, whereas if a person is more narcissistic, it will be counterproductive because they feel demeaned.

Reiss also said that those who have lower self-esteem could end up feeling as if they don't deserve any attention, which will trigger anxiety or guilt that could end up being counterproductive. The average person and those with mild narcissistic tendencies will thrive with attention. Those who have a severe narcissistic personality or are antisocial will often react in a smug way and feel as if it was about time that they were recognized, which may cause resentment, a reaction to "rest on their laurels" once they receive attention, and then "ease up" instead of being motivated.

Everybody dreads to hear the term "busy work." Among Americans, the definition of busy work means projects or assignments that are used to waste time but are in no way productive or constructive. This is common in education, but it can happen just as often in the workplace.

The issue with busy work, besides the fact that employees will become frustrated and their morale will suffer is that many will confuse busy work with productivity. Even if this kind of work causes urgency, it doesn't necessarily mean that it is productive work. While productivity can help you overcome procrastination, knowing the difference between productivity and busy work is important. If you allow yourself to become burned out by busy work, you will be more likely to procrastinate on the important work. We're going to take a quick look at what are non-productive tasks like updating or reading social media, holding meetings, and checking emails. While these tasks could be important, they are endless and time-consuming.

Take this scenario for example. A person can sort through over 200 emails in less than 15 minutes if they need to, so why is that it will take hours each day for them to check half as many if they don't have to.

They come to the conclusion that by accepting an email, you allow it to be an interruption and you stop something that was productive. You are working on getting something done, almost completely finish, and *ding* an email. You look. It's from your grandma, boss, or colleague. You quit everything and respond.

All of these tiny little interruptions will mess with your focus and concentration, and if you let this happen several times during the day, it can have a large impact on your level of productivity. To be productive and not busy, you need to:

Cure for the Procrastination Puzzle

- Stay off social media.

- Stop "staying updated" on blogs and news.

- Keep meetings short or avoid them altogether.

- Minimize the amount of time you spend on your phone.

- Check your emails only a couple of times during the day.

However, there are a lot of jobs where constantly using social media all day and perusing blogs for trends is completely normal and even expected. These types of workers and those who work a lot on computers could be a part of an increasing number of digital-age employees who have more than one computer. Whether you work at home or in an office, multiple monitors will allow the person to look at several data streams by shifting an eye.

There are studies that have found that multiple monitors are able to help with productivity. Still, there are experts that think that it will all depend on the work and the characteristics of the person using the computer.

Reiss believes that the psychological effect that multiple monitors have on a person is that they are going to feel more important, which will help their self-esteem, create a sense of respect, and will improve motivation and productivity.

Diet and Nutrition

Nutrition and diet play a large part in a person's lifestyle. The kinds of food that people eat, how much they eat, and what time they eat factor directly and indirectly into productivity.

Some people argue that breakfast is the "most important meal of the day." Experts think that breakfast will help provide a person with glucose which provides you with energy. Since you can't eat while you sleep, your glucose levels drop and having breakfast in the morning will allow the body to create simple sugars that your bloodstream absorbs where it then heads to the cells for energy.

This is why experts believe that skipping breakfast isn't a good idea since you could lose some valuable productive hours until they eat their first meal.

Exercise

Everybody knows that exercise can improve your health, but it can also improve your productivity. According to Ingeborg Grabow, "Exercising releases endorphins in the brain." These endorphins are chemicals that your body produces due to some stimuli and can originate in many different areas which include the spinal cord, pituitary gland, and other areas of the nervous system and brain.

According to Grabow, "Exercising four times a week for approximately 20 to 30 minutes is the equivalent of 20 milligrams of Prozac." Exercising also has the ability to de-stress you, it gives you a break, and clears your mind. All of this can boost and increase productivity.

Physical and Mental Health
How productive you are will often depend on your circumstances and factors like disability and illness. For example, people who have OCD or who suffer from anxiety will often recheck the work they do which can drag out their productivity. Their tendency to become overwhelmed or stressed can hurt their productivity, even if their work is more accurate due to their slower performance. Reiss has broken down the psychological factors that can influence a person's productivity:

Sincerity – There are a certain amount of people with antisocial tendencies and overly manipulative people who would see an injury as a chance to misuse and manipulate the disability system.

Work enjoyment/peer relationships – People who enjoy what they do and get along with their colleagues will find more motivation to get back to normal functioning. Those who don't like their work or are uncomfortable with their colleagues will often feel taken advantage of. They will see an injury as a way out.

Family dynamics – Reiss found that there are two different types of families: those who tend to overreact and overcompensate to a person who is sick or injured and provide more caring and attention than they would normally get, thus creating an unconscious motivation to stay in an injured role, and the dysfunctional family type who reacts in a hostile or negative way to the injured party and view them as worthless or useless. The latter type may sometimes motivate the person to "get better" more often, it will cause them to act defensively to prove that they are injured.

The productivity level of a person can be influenced by several different psychological factors. With the society in the US so productivity focused, knowing the best way to improve it can be extremely valuable and can be helpful to your overall wellbeing and health.

Chapter 5:
The Importance of Motivation

Motivation is important to everybody. Motivation helps us live. There is no way to live our lives happily if we don't have motivation. Motivation means that you have desires and purpose to achieve your daily life, business, and career goals. Motivation is what helps us to wake up earlier and be productive.

When we get more than we expect from something, are inspired, or excited is what helps us to become motivated. It inspires people when they read beliefs and stories of those who are successful. It inspires them when they can see a person feel happy and achieve something great. This is how we get motivated and it will end up helping us to reach our goals.

You can find a bunch of motivational things in the world like motivation from teachers, parents, kids, trees, water, seminar, quotes, and books. But we aren't able to find all of them.

The reason for this is because we aren't connected with motivation. Motivation is a sense that is able to reach our mind and heart equally throughout the day, but for a lot of us, we fail to get it. Having a sense of motivation is important to several different life achievements.

What Is Motivation?

Motivation is defined as having the will to accomplish something. It works as a psychological force that makes you want to do something. This is a cognition and impression that can end up happening accidentally at any time during the night or day. We get the best amount of motivation when our purpose and motivation meet up. For example, motivational videos can activate your sense of motivation and it will start to connect with your sense of purpose. This is the reason why people will often watch these types of videos and why so many people recommend watching motivational speeches and stories. Motivation will help you to achieve dreams and goals in your business, career, and life.

It can also be said that motivation is the reason or the intent behind something. Why is it that you want to learn? Why is it you like to write? There are reasons behind all of your actions. One of these reasons is going to be a motive.

Another view of motivation is seen in Steven Press field's definition of motivation. He describes motivation as "At some point, the pain of not doing it becomes greater than the pain of doing it." In other words, you will reach a point where it will be easier to change than to stay the same.

This is a very basic definition of motivation. Each choice that is made will come with some sort of price, but when a person becomes motivated, it will be easier for them to handle the inconvenience of taking action than the pain that they will experience if they do nothing.

The funny thing about motivation is that it will often come once you have started your new behavior and not before. Motivation is a normal result of some form of action and not the cause of the action. Getting started on something, even if it is very small, is a type of active inspiration that will provide you with natural momentum.

Why We Need Motivation

It's important that we have motivation in order to live a flexible, happy, and wealthy life. Motivation will help us to manage our time efficiently. Motivation will help you to manage your daily life challenges, time, and opportunities to help you to move forward and achieve your goals.

Motivation will help you to manage your time and you will become more beneficial and productive for organizations. Here's an example, official, personal dreams and goals will motivate you to wake up earlier. You do yoga and cardio in order to remain fit and healthy. This is because you are working your way towards your goals.

When you feel motivated, you aren't going to want to waste your time. You will communicate based on facts and values. You will be able to focus on the things you have to get done by the end of the day. This is the reason why motivated people tend to be more productive and use their time more wisely.

There are many people who struggle to find their motivation to achieve their goals because they waste all of their energy and time on other areas. If you are interested in making it easy to find motivation and get started on your projects, then you have to automate the early sections of your behavior.

Motivation Can Make You A Better Manager

Everybody has been an employee at some point and I'm sure you don't like negative and lazy mindsets in your leaders or managers. This is the reason why motivation in the workplace matters the most for the leaders and managers. The reason for this is that teammates or employees are able to be less excited to work or negative about projects, but managers and leaders show that they value the project, are excited, creative, and energized.

Motivation will help the business make their employees motivated and happy so that they work hard towards their goals. In order to help increase the motivation levels of employees, businesses and organizations will promote, honor publicly, increase the salary, appreciate, and provide facilities to those who deserve it.

This will help to connect the sense of purpose and sense of motivation in their employee's minds. They will then dedicate hours of their time to achieve the goals of the organization.

This is the reason why motivation will help you to become more productive at work. While there are some employees that can self-motivate and understand when they reach what they are working for, there are people who aren't. If you are in charge of a team of employees, then make sure you talk with them nicely, appreciate all of the efforts, don't focus on their mistakes, and focus on developing them and respecting their feelings and viewpoints.

Never ever make them feel as if they are less than in anything. You should motivate them and inspire them. These motivational practices will improve the morale of your workers and they will find more motivation. This is the reason why motivation within a business is imperative for any form of productivity.

Motivation in Schools

Motivation is also extremely important for students and teachers. Teachers who are motivated will be able to inspire students to stay focused. Students who are motivated to learn will help to inspire their teachers. Teaching is very much a selfless act.

When it comes to teaching, there is no motivation in the salary. Many teachers in India teach children for free or at a very minimum wage. They don't find motivation in the salary of their job. They find motivation in exploring the creativity in their students. They find motivation in putting smiles on the faces of their students. They find motivation in building their career. They train their students to fight any life and career problems.

Students aren't going to feel very motivated to get an advanced degree when they know that there aren't many jobs for existing degree holders. Teachers aren't going to be very motivated when their government isn't supporting them.

This is the reason why it is so important for students and teachers to be motivated and it's because they are country developers. If these types of people aren't motivated, then you will notice that it takes several more years to develop.

Motivation in Life

Motivation is important for a successful life. Humans are faced with millions of obstacles every single day. A few of these obstacles are caused by natural disaster out of our control and some are caused by an uneducated society and impractical government laws and policies.

Let's say a farmer's crops are destroyed by flooding then this becomes an obstacle in their life. Their hopes and efforts could disappear. Now the farmer will have to become motivated to try things again and if they don't find the motivation, they won't be able to get things going again. Another obstacle they could end up experiencing is not being able to pay off their bank loan because they are getting lower prices for their crops and so on.

There are many different types of problems and obstacles that we will have to face day after day. Some lose hope and think about giving up.

But when we are able to provide our self with a motivational environment, our sense of purpose will become activated. If we were to attend a motivational seminar or if we read a motivational book, we could increase our motivational environment. If we were the farmer that lost their crops, we could find inspirational stories about others who had gone through the same or similar experience. This would renew our sense of purpose so that we would try again.

To really live, you have to have the hunger to do so.

Motivation in Sports

Why is it that sports players tend to be healthier and more fit than other people in the country? This is because they exercise on a daily basis. The reason for this is because their sense of purpose is strong. They know they have fans and the entire country expecting them to win, and they know that staying physically active and healthy will help them win.

Their motivation for exercising is what others expect from them, their goals, and their desires to reach their dreams, as well as having the hunger to win. This is the reason why motivation is so important.

Motivation in Nursing

Nursing, similar to teaching, is done with the expectations of a high salary. There may be some that go into for the money, but nursing tends to be a career choice for those who want to help people. It requires heart for a person to be a nurse and care for people unconditionally. It may be a hard work, but for the right person, it can be extremely satisfying for their happiness and soul. With no motivation, it would be extremely hard to stay a nurse based solely on the salary.

Motivation for Salespeople

Nearly 90% of businesses will give their employees bonuses or incentives for reaching sales goals or creating leads. Promotions, salary, and bonuses have a way of motivating teams to make more sales.

The reason they get motivated is that they get more money once they achieve their goals. They understand that they will be able to use the money they get for their family and personal development. This is the reason why salespeople have all of the motivation they need to sell things.

Getting A Job

It is possible to get a job offer on the first go, but if you don't, what is going to make you try again. It's a sense of purpose, its reasons, its motivation, it's your desires, and dreams that motivate you to continue trying, trying, and trying. And it's the reason why you keep from repeating your mistakes. You can see this all over the world. People get jobs, work, or projects even after hundreds of rejections.

Life can be very difficult for dreamers. Everybody will struggle and we all do. The reason for this is that we have desires and jobs that motivate us to work through these rough times, and to keeping pushing through to our final destination until we take our last breath. This is why motivation helps people to get a job.

There are a lot of reasons why motivation is important for our daily life, but I think you get the picture. Motivation is what can make you smile and feel happy with your life. Motivation is what helps you to master your skills. Motivation helps improve innovation. Motivation is what helps you to achieve your career goals. Motivation is what helps you make healthy habits. Motivation is what will help you to live a successful life.

Chapter 6:
The Impact of Willpower and Self-Discipline

Self-Discipline or willpower is a very important and useful skill that everybody needs to have. It is an essential skill to have in every area of your life, and while most people know that it is important, very few of them will do anything to strengthen it.

Contrary to popular belief, self-discipline doesn't mean you have to be mean with yourself or keep up a limited and restrictive lifestyle. Self-discipline merely means that you have self-control, which shows that you have inner strength and can control yourself, your reactions, and your actions when you need to.

Specifically, self-discipline is the ability to control your behaviors, reactions, emotions, and impulses. It lets you forego short-term gratification so that you can reach long-term gain and satisfaction. It's the ability to say no when all you really want to do is say yes. It doesn't mean you have to lead a boring and restrictive life void of any enjoyment. In fact, it is nearly impossible to be completely self-disciplined in every area of your life. Instead, it could be used to help you focus on what is the most important to you.

Self-discipline is what gives you the power to stick to the decisions you make and see them through without changing your choices. This is why it is important when it comes to achieving your goals. Possessing this skill will enable you to persevere with your plans and decisions until you have reached your goal. It will also show up in your inner strength, helping you to work through laziness, addictions, and procrastination so that you can follow through with anything you want to do.

A common characteristic of willpower is being able to reject the need for instant pleasure and gratification so that you can have a greater gain. This will require spending time and effort to get to it. Self-discipline is one of the key components of success. It can be seen in several different ways such as:

- Trying something over and over again until you have accomplished what you wanted to do.
- The ability to resist temptations and distractions.
- Self-control.

- The ability to not give up even though you experience setbacks and failures.

- Perseverance.

Life will put problems and challenges on your path to achievement and success and for you to rise above them, you are going to have to act with persistence and perseverance and this is going to require you to have self-discipline.

Having willpower will lead to self-esteem and self-confidence and as a result, we lead to satisfaction and happiness. On the other hand, if you lack self-discipline, it can lead to obesity, relationship and health problems, loss, failure, and many other problems.

Possessing self-discipline can also help you to overcome negative habits like drinking, smoking, addictions, and eating disorders. You will also be able to make yourself study more, exercise every day, create new skills, and improve yourself, and grow your spirituality.

As I stated earlier, the majority of people know the benefits and importance of self-discipline, but most of them won't do anything to improve it. However, you can improve this ability just like all other skills. This can be done through exercises and training.

Importance and Benefits

Having self-discipline can help you:

- Meditate on a regular basis.

- Start a book and finish reading it.

- Overcome the habit of watching too much television.

- Wake up earlier in the morning.

- Continue to work on your diet and resist the temptation of eating foods that are bad for you.

- Head to the gym, go for a walk, or a swim even if your mind is telling you to sit at home and binge watch Netflix.

- Continue to work on your project even after your initial enthusiasm has disappeared.

- Overcome procrastination and laziness.

- Fulfill the promises you made to yourself and others.

- Avoid acting in a rash way or on impulses.

The Marshmallow Study

Cure for the Procrastination Puzzle

Over 40 years ago, psychologist Walter Michel, Ph.D. explored self-control in children through a very simple but extremely effective test. He called his experiment the "marshmallow test" and it created the groundwork for our current study of self-control.

Michel and his fellow researchers gave a preschooler a plate that had a treat on it like a marshmallow. The child was then informed that the researcher was going to step out of the room for a few minutes but not before that gave the child a choice. If they will be able to wait for the researcher to return, they would get two treats. If they will not be able to wait, they could ring a bell to call the researcher back in but they could only have the one treat.

Willpower in children and adults can be viewed as the ability to delay gratification. Certain kids have good self-control in order to let go of the immediate joy of eating a treat so that they can indulge in two treats later on. Ex-smokers are able to give up the joy of cigarette so that they can have good health and avoid a higher risk of lung cancer. Shoppers are able to resist the urge to splurge so that they can save for retirement.

Through the marshmallow study, Michel and his colleagues created the framework to explain how humans can delay gratification. He came up with what he referred to as "hot-and-cool" systems that explained if willpower would fail or succeed. The cool system is cognitive and is the thinking system. It incorporates goals, actions, feelings, and sensations. It reminds you why you should wait to eat the treat. The hot system is emotional and impulsive. The hot system is what causes you to respond quickly and reflexively such as throwing the treat in your mouth without thinking about what it could do.

If your willpower fails, it will expose your hot stimulus causing it to override the cool which causes you to act impulsively. Everybody has a different susceptible to these hot triggers. Your susceptibility to emotional responses could have an influence on your life. When Michel revisited the children, who participated in the marshmallow study after they become adolescents, he discovered that those who had been able to wait longer scored higher on the SATs and their parents often rated them as having a good ability at responding with reason, handling stress, planning, and exhibited good self-control in frustrating situations.

It didn't end there. A new set of researchers tracked down the children, now in the 40s, and tested their willpower with lab tasks to see how their self-control was as an adult. Amazingly, their willpower had held up for more than four decades. Those children who hadn't fared well in the task as a child did poorly on the self-control tasks as an adult. It seems that a person's sensitivity to hot stimuli may persist through their life.

They also looked the brain activity in some of their subjects with functional magnetic resonance imaging. They presented them with what was considered tempting stimuli, and the individuals who didn't have much self-control exhibited brain patterns that were different than those who had high self-control. They discovered that the prefrontal cortex would be more active in those who had better self-control. The ventral striatum had more activity in those who had less self-control. Research has yet to figure out completely why there are some that are more sensitive to emotional temptation and triggers and if these types of patterns could be corrected.

Stephen Patterson

Chapter 7:
Overcoming Procrastination

It's Friday afternoon and you can hear the clock ticking. You are working like a madman to get a task finished before your five o'clock deadline, while you also curse yourself for not getting started on it sooner.

How could you let this happen? Where did everything go wrong? Why did you end of losing focus?

Well, there are all those hours that you spend reading through your emails and checking in on social media. All of the "preparation," coffee breaks, and the time you spend doing other things that could have been left for you to do next week. Does this sound familiar? Well, you're not alone.

Many of us fall into the trap of procrastination from time to time. In fact, according to Piers Steel, a speaker, and researcher, 95% of the population will procrastinate to some degree. While it is probably comforting to realize that you are not alone, it can also be sobering to know that you are holding yourself back a lot.

Does Procrastination Mean You Are Being Lazy?

Laziness and procrastination are often confused, but they are actually very different. Procrastination is a process that is active. This means that you choose to do something else instead of doing the thing that you know you need to do. In contrast, laziness most often suggests that there is some form of apathy, unwillingness, and inactivity.

Procrastination means that you ignoring an unpleasant but important task, in favor of doing something that is easier or more enjoyable. When you give into these impulses, it can have some serious consequences. For example, minor episodes of procrastination can end up causing you to feel ashamed or guilty. It can end up leading to a reduction of productivity and can cause you to miss out on reaching your goals.

If you procrastinate for a long time, you could end up becoming disillusioned and demotivated with your work, which could end up leading to depression or the loss of your job.

As with all habits, it is completely possible for you to overcome procrastination. The last 12 chapters will each teach you a new trick to overcome your procrastination. But the first thing you need to do is to realize when you are procrastinating. You can have all the tricks in the world to overcome it, but if you can't recognize when you're doing it, they aren't going to be all that effective.

You could end up putting off a task because you have had to re-prioritize all of your work. If you briefly delay something important for an actual good reason, then this doesn't necessarily mean you are procrastinating. However, if you continue to put things off indefinitely or you change your focus because you want to avoid completing something, then you are probably procrastinating. You could also be procrastinating if you realize you are:

- Filling up your day with tasks that have low-priority.

- Keep an item on your To-Do list for a really long time even though it is extremely important.

- You read through your emails several times throughout the day without making a decision on what you're going to do with them.

- You begin your high-priority task and then you head off to make coffee.

- You fill up your time with a bunch of unimportant tasks that other people have asked you to do, instead of getting the important things that you have written on your list.

- You wait until you are in the "right mood" or you are waiting for the "best time" to take care of your task.

Once you have realized you are procrastinating, try using one of the tricks below to stop procrastinating. You can also use these tricks before you start procrastinating, which will end up saving you time in the long run.

Chapter 8:
Figure Out the Reason for Your Procrastination

Earlier in this book, we talked about several different reasons for procrastination. One of the most common questions that a therapist will hear is, "Why do I always procrastinate even though I know it will cause me anxiety?" You know everything that you need to do, but you don't do it or you allow yourself to wait until the last minute to do it. Over and over again you do this. The pattern will continue to repeat. You start feeling caught and trapped in this vortex of procrastination, anxiety, and stress.

A lot of procrastinators have been told or they tell themselves that the reason they procrastinate is that they are lazy, disorganize, or worse, because they don't care. For the most part, there could be nothing further from the truth. Procrastinators tend to be hardworking, capable, and smart people, they just really have a hard time getting things done when they are supposed to and they don't know why.

If you find yourself often wondering about the reasons why you procrastinate, let's take a little quiz to see if any of these sounds familiar. I want you to ask yourself the following questions:

- When you have a task to do, do you start thinking of the different ways that it could go wrong?

- Do you start picturing how all of the important people around you could react if you end up failing?

- Do you find yourself thinking that it's better that you not even try than to do your best and end up failing?

- Do you find yourself overwhelmed by the possibility of your new responsibilities if you end up being successful?

- Do you believe the idea of "If I do well, then other people will expect me to do more"?

- Do you often feel that your success is going to lead other people knowing who the "real you" are?

- Do you think that if you have to do something that you have to do it perfectly?

- Do you often find it hard to persist when things don't end up going just right?

- Would you rather not do something than end up doing it imperfectly?

Your answers to these questions are able to tell you a lot about the reasons behind your procrastination.
For questions one through three, if you answered yes, then your reason for procrastination could be fear of failure. The thought of putting your effort into something but failing creates a feeling of anxiousness, so you decide to avoid doing it. By doing this, when your project does fail, you are able to rationalize that it wasn't really a test of your true abilities, you needed more time.

For questions four through six, if you answer yes, then your reason for procrastination is a fear of success. Procrastination is able to protect you from greater responsibilities and higher expectations that could come along with succeeding. Like the ones who procrastinate because they don't want to fail, you will keep yourself safe from facing all of your true limits by staying away from challenges and putting things off.

For questions seven through nine, if you answered yes, your reason for procrastination could be perfectionism. Because you have the belief that things have to be done perfectly, the result will be that nothing ever gets done. When you have to face a task, you will find yourself becoming overwhelmed and frustrated by your own impossible standards.

While each person's reasons for procrastination will vary, the results will often be the same — an endless cycle of avoidance, anxiety, and shame. You don't ever get anything done and you aren't able to enjoy anything in your life with all of the guilt that hangs over your head. You might play some golf instead of working on the presentation that you need but the image of frowning boss nags at you during your game. You aren't able to relax because you will always have something else that you need to be doing. Procrastination won't work for anybody because avoidance isn't going to get rid of anxiety, it only delays it.

The great thing is that there are many different effective strategies that can help you overcome procrastination and anxiety. By using the tricks in this book, you will be able to learn skills to help you decrease your avoidance and help control your anxiety.

Chapter 9:
Audit Your Goals Weekly

If you are really determined to get your procrastination under control and your life in order, then all you need to grab is a sharpie, a few post-it notes, a wall, and a couple of hours of free time. We are going to do what is known as a life audit. This will help you create a starting point for accomplishing things in a timely manner. If you don't know what your goals are, then you won't be able to figure out where you need to start.

An illustrator and writer, Ximena Vennochi detailed the why and the how of a life audit. It's important that you take some time to check in with yourself so that you can see how you are doing, what you are doing, and what has become important that wasn't important in the past. A life audit can help you figure this out.

Basically, a life audit means that you are organizing your life and being completely honest with yourself.

- First, you are going to write down all of your goals, hopes, and life necessities on post-it notes. This could be owning a home near the ocean, getting a new job, or winning an award for your writing.

- Second, you will organize your post-its by category as you start to notice your themes. This could be career, health, family, and so on.

- Third, you will organize them by time. This means how long it is going to take you to accomplish that task.

The really big life audit doesn't have to be done every single week. You can do the big life audit if you find yourself stuck in a rut, every month, or once a year. What you should do every week is to look over the goals that you can do, work towards and accomplish in that single week. Doing this, especially when you feel like you don't know what to do, is a great way to help you accomplish things.

Here's the process:

- Your goal is to write out 100 post-in an hour.

Take your post-it notes and write out 100 "wishes" on each one. These could be any sort of goal or wish that you would like. There is not a single wish that is too big or too small. This could take a while, but brainstorm until you have come up with at least 100 wishes.

There are a lot of people who tend to stop at around 30 to 40 post-its. They think they have run out of things that they would like to do or accomplish, and they often feel relieved by that. They believe that the smaller number of goals they have, the more within reach it will be.

If you can really only come up with 30 to 40 post-it, that's fine. Don't be hard on yourself. But I would really like for you to try and reach 100 wishes. This will really let you know who you are. They don't have to be simple things like getting a raise, working out every day, and so on. You need to think big. Think about the places you would like to travel. Things that you have always wanted to do. Have a glass of wine and get creative. You should feel excited about writing these things down because you have likely ignored many of these wants. Now you are accepting the things that you really want to do.

- If you blow past 100 post- in an hour, that's fine. It's also okay if it takes you longer than an hour to write down 100 wishes.

You have now finished your initial brainstorm.

Next, you will sort your post-its and group them into wish themes. Three simple categories could be creative, personal, and professional. This could get a bit confusing as you could easily place every single note under personal. Everything that you want to do should come from some personal place. So, you shouldn't use a personal category. You need to get more specific.

This will likely take you some time to figure out all of your categories. You will probably have to group and regroup until you really figure something out. You may even be surprised by some of the categories you come up with and how many wishes fall into certain categories. Now, if there is a category that you felt came out a little low, it might not mean anything bad. Chances are that category is so close to your heart that you aren't worried about not doing things that fall into that category. It's something that you easily make time for already. At this point, you may need to take a little break because we're going to get more specific.

You will need to plot your wishes by time. You should have a pretty good idea as to what you want and there is probably a lot of stuff going on. You are probably feeling overwhelmed and unsure of where you should start. By sorting these wishes further into a spectrum of when will help to ease this feeling.

Cure for the Procrastination Puzzle

When you do this, the category they are in doesn't matter. Some of your goals will affect your life every single day and won't be a onetime thing. Alright, so you have three timeframes you will sort things into:

- Now or Soon – these are wishes that can be done immediately but will need some sort of prioritization or steps.

- Someday – these wishes are long-term goals and milestone moments.

- Always or Every Day – these are wishes that will need deliberate actions that you do every single day.

Now, if you want, you can be more specific with some of your wishes and write a due date. I feel the three categories will be easier for most people to handle than having to get really specific.
Now, look at your categories you found in step two through the lens of your timeframes. Mark each post-it with something that symbolizes the timeframes. You will be able to see things more clearly.

Your priorities should have naturally surfaced. The important thing is to notice if your breakdown aligns with the way you are currently spending your time.

Next, you need to perform your five activities. This means that you need to write down the five activities that you spend the most time on. Sorting them into a pie chart to represent how much time you spend on each as compared to the others will help you to see where you need to spend your time.

If work takes up a large portion of your chart but you want to make time for other things, then you may want to take work off of your chart. Change your breakdown to show how you spend your time on things you like doing other than your work. This will show you if you are spending the right amount of time in the areas that correlate with your wishes that you created earlier. You may need to rebalance some things.

Now, you have finished your big life audit. This may seem like a lot of work to overcome procrastination, but if you are able to direct your focus on certain goals, you will be less likely to procrastinate.

The next thing you can do is make all of this digital. Put the things you wrote down and the timeframes into a spreadsheet or document of some sort. This way you can pull it up whenever you do another big life audit and compare the results and see how you are faring. Those post-its aren't going to stay on your wall forever.

Here comes the weekly audit. What you need to do is look at your spreadsheet and figure out which goals you are able to do in the following week. Write those down and work toward those for the next seven days.

The next week, do the same thing. See how many goals you accomplished the week before and add new ones for your next week. This will keep you focused and working towards your overall good.

Stephen Patterson

Chapter 10:
Get Rid of Negative Self-Talk

Having some self-criticism is okay. It can be a good reality check that will spur you to become better, but there is a big difference between "I need to exercise more" and calling yourself fat.

Too much self-criticism will often backfire because you will start to focus on your "failures" instead of the little things that you can do to improve yourself. Self-trash-talk over a long period of time is associated with depression and stress. Let's look at how to shut up your inner critic.

1.Place Your Negative Things in A Box.
You will often blow things out of proportion when you are beating yourself up. The next time this happens, take a few deep breaths and narrow down your negative thought into a tiny little box. Visualize a tiny box and this will tell you that the problem isn't that big and help you to feel more confident.

2. Possible Thinking Power.
A lot of people think that they have to think positively. But some research suggests when you are feeling down, thinking positive can make you feel worse. You should try possible thinking. This means finding a neutral thought about something.

3. Find Out If You're Really Guilty.
If you accidentally blurt out that your Spanx is too tight, you may think that you have made a fool of yourself, but have you really? Did they all recoil in horror or were they messing with their phone under the table and not paying attention. Ask yourself some follow up questions to figure out how bad the situation actually is.

4. Ask Yourself What Your Friend Would Do.
Your friends are your confidants and won't be as harsh with you as you are to yourself. The next time you feel nasty self-talk coming on, think of a person you trust and think about what they would tell you. Also, if you are able to tell yourself something that you would never say to your friend, then you don't need to tell it to yourself.

5. Name Your Inner Critic.

A silly name works the best. It's going to be hard to take your inner voice seriously if its name was The Swamp Monster.

6.Call Somebody.
Shame can only work if you keep it to yourself. If you have done something that you think was stupid, grab your phone and speak it out loud. This act will cut the shame off at the knees. When you tell somebody about it, chances are, the two of you will laugh about it.

Stephen Patterson

Chapter 11:
Focus on a Single Task

Being able to do only one thing at a time is a great way of being very productive. When you think about it, it doesn't make sense. Aren't we supposed to do more in order to be productive? Nope, it isn't. When you do more than one thing is a great way to be busier and it sometimes is a more engaging way to work. When we do multiple things at once, our brains get more stimulated and it will release dopamine which is a pleasure chemical. Studies have shown that even though multitasking is stimulating, it might make us feel productive, but it actually makes us less productive.

The amount of attention that we give to what is in front of us is very limited. Each moment of each day, our brains get flooded with tasks, thoughts, words, sounds, sights, and more. It only has the ability to focus on so much. One study done found that our brains receive over 11 million pieces of information every second but it is only able to process 40 of them. Wow, that is a big difference. We have to learn to invest our attention wisely.

What is even more surprising is studies have shown that when we think we are multitasking, we really aren't. It is not possible for our brains to be able to focus on two things at one time. It is switching rapidly between them. Instead of channeling our energy and focus into just one task, we are spreading ourselves too thin. This keeps us from diving into any of our tasks. When multitasking, we are doing a poor job of everything.

Even though this is true, we can't deny that when we multitask, it makes us feel incredible. This is the main reason we do it. Multitasking will make us less productive in many different ways. Multitasking makes each task longer to accomplish. We can't ignore irrelevant information. It makes it harder for us to organize and store information. It can even affect our memory. When we multitask, our brains automatically go into auto-pilot mode. This makes it harder to remember what we have worked on. This is why when we are watching television with our computers on our lap, we don't remember what was on the television.

The Drawbacks
There is a lot of evidence that multitasking is very counterproductive. Multitasking being powerful is nothing but a myth. Humans are a single

core processor. We cannot take notes, listen to somebody asking for feedback, and check our emails at the same time. Sure, we can do it, but not effectively. When we juggle tasks, it increases the amount of time we spend trying to refocus on tasks and divides our attention. It gives people the impression that we are focusing on them and essentially, we aren't. It will also rob you of focus that you could be directing toward a more important task.

Hang on, it gets worse. Multitasking can be harmful to our mental and physical health and reduces our ability to make decisions. Multitasking drains our brains and exhausts our minds. It can zap cognitive resources and if it goes unchecked, it can cause us to decreased sharpness and mental decline. People who constantly multitask will have increased level of the stress hormone cortisol and this can damage our memory.

Now, is multitasking still something you would like to perfect? Don't be surprised if you miss goals, make errors, and get burnt out.

Single-Tasking
This is the complete opposite of multitasking. It is better in every way possible. We might try to resist single tasking because it doesn't stimulate our brains. When we work on only one task at a time, we can go

deeper and do the task better. By doing it this way, we aren't spreading our energy, attention, and time among many things. Single-tasking allows us to create more space around our work at any given moment. This allows us to be more creative, make better connections, think deeper, and find more meaning with our work.

If you can remember your last productive day, you weren't doing many things at one time. You were probably working on only one task and spending a lot of time, energy, and attention on it. It will take energy and time to adapt to not being stimulated during the day, but it will be worth it.

Single-tasking even lets us build our attention muscles. This is how much control we have over where our attention gets directed. A study shows that around 47 percent of our time is spent thinking about things that are unrelated to what is in front of our faces. A person who is more attentive will be more productive than a person who only focuses on their work about 50 percent of the time. Single-tasking can help us strengthen our attention muscle since each time we bring our attention back to what we are doing, we are working our attention muscle and this develops our executive function.

Let's compare time with money. You are shopping and you found a shirt and a pair of jeans that cost $20 each. You only have $20 so you can't buy both of them. We can accept this as a basic truth when talking about money, but when we think about time, we can't comprehend the same concept. This is just silly. If two different projects are going to take you two hours each and you need to focus on each of them, we can't do them in the same two hours.

If you think about it, time is more valuable than money since it is scarcer. You can increase the amount of money you get each week, month, and year and many of us do. You can't do this with time. We only have a certain amount in every day, month, and year. Instead of adding time in our days, the best we can do is decrease the amount we take to do the things we need to do each day.

Just like any resource, if we can't figure out how to increase it, our only choice is to manage what we have. This means we have to budget. Yes, I said, budget our time.

We have to diligently track our time just like we track our money. If you are familiar with budgets, before you can efficiently budget, you have to understand your spending habits. When you know where your money is going, you can understand how to manage it. This holds true for time. Many of us have only a vague idea of what happens to our time.

There are apps that help you track your time by client, project, and task. They are easy to use. They will make reports, edits categories, and entries. The best benefit for tracking time is that it will almost immediately stop all distractions. You probably have a mindset that every morning you have to check your social media, email, and wait you need to check on that thing your significant other wanted to buy. When you use a time tracking app before beginning a project, it will be easier to keep yourself focused on just one thing. It will help you stay focused on just one thing at a time.

You will be amazed that you won't be checking your emails constantly. You will begin telling friends, family, and coworkers that you can't be bothered during certain hours. Your focus will increase drastically and you will be moving toward your larger goals.

If you aren't a person who likes using apps, no need to worry. All you need is a timer. Do you believe me that it is that simple? Try it for one week. You need to set a timer for 20 minutes. This is the amount of time you are able to concentrate on a single task before you lose focus. Use this time and only do one thing. Your brain may resist in the beginning but when you have settled into the groove of things, you are going to feel incredible. After the 20 minutes are up, think about how much you were able to accomplish in just 20 minutes. You are going to be amazed.

Because we are giving what we do a name and a specified amount of time, we will be more invested in getting it finished. You will spend your time on it instead of letting it slip between your fingers without doing anything. You will be singularly focused on what you are doing when you do it, and then you will see the benefits of single-tasking just because you are accountable for every minute of every hour you work.

Productivity doesn't measure how busy you are or how quickly you work. It is about what we accomplish. This is what we are left with at the end of the day. Doing just one thing at a time is the best way to accomplish more in less time.

Stephen Patterson

Chapter 12:
Time Chunking

Do you always have multiple tabs open on your computer? At the end of your day, can you positively show that any task has been completed that was on your task list?

Not to worry. You are among millions of other people that are constantly distracted by all the notifications, alerts, and dings that pop up on all your devices during the day. If you are beginning to feel unproductive by all the things you can't seem to get done, here are some ways to learn how to time chunk to help you stay productive and focused.

What Is Time Chunking?
A simple definition of chunking is grouping information together in small enough pieces so you can use them efficiently to get the outcome you would like without shutting down or getting stressed. The main source of stress in our lives happen when we feel like we have so many things to do and never enough time to get them all done. We

make to-do lists, but then get overwhelmed before we can even start the list.

When we are constantly bombarded with many different streams of information, we can't pay attention to everything at one time. We can't control our memories or go from one task to the next, as well as others who like completing one task at a time.

We will take one task and pull it into millions of pieces or place it together in an abstract whole. Let's say you are on a project trying to do the entire thing at one time, you will become overwhelmed fairly quickly. Just as its counterpart, if you take a project and turn it into a lot of small steps, it will be equally frustrating, daunting, and overwhelming. How can we fix this?

It might be best to learn how to time chunk. By doing this, we are organizing all of our tasks into one so we won't lose productivity or focus when going between tasks. You can organize this by days or hours. You might want to write on Monday and save your social media and email for another day you aren't as busy.

You could also chunk the tasks into hours during your day. If you are in sales, you could take your mornings and do cold calls and your afternoons could be spent answering emails. If you don't know which one would be best for you, try some different variations and settle on what makes you feel more productive. When we say productive, it means the one that helped you reach your goals.

Many people are only able to focus on a certain number of things at once. When a person is learning, they have a tendency to remember things better if they are grouped into groups of three. Groups larger than three are just too hard for us to remember. Basically, we will get overwhelmed after three separate chunks of information.

When we can't reach our goals, it is not because we aren't able to. It is due to the way we focus on the items or the way we are chunking items. When we can take everything that comes at us and put them into ideal sized groups that we can handle, we are helping ourselves accomplish our goals.

Begin with Capturing

To start the process of chunking, you have to get your ideas out of your head and put them on paper, your cell phone, tablet, or computer. This process is called capturing.

When we keep everything in our minds, we are just adding more stress. We have to create a habit where we write things down that we need to accomplish. We are only humans and can only focus on a certain number of tasks at one time. We can usually handle between five to nine tasks at one time.

Write down the communications, meetings, and ideas you have to do and what you need to do in order to accomplish each one. Write down the tasks that you absolutely have to do. It might be something you want such as that job promotion or other things that are demanding your attention such as taking your child to basketball practice or that laundry that is piling up on the floor. Write down every single thing you have to accomplish this week. Think about this as a dumping ground for all of your thoughts.

Goals

Time chunking is useless when you don't have any goals tied to your tasks. You need to be sure you know what outcome organizing your time will accomplish. Without knowing, you may just miss the whole point and begin frantically responding to all notifications.

If you react to each thing that grabs your attention, you are not going to be productive at all. You are going to need something bigger to keep you on task. This is where goals come in to play. You need to create goals that relate to completed tasks or money or both. These goals also help guide your plan that helps you reach your productivity levels.

Planning Chunks

After you have your goals, you are going to want to create tasks in order to help you reach them. This is your plan. If you have a goal of reaching a certain number of sales for this quarter, you will need to work backward and find what activities will get you to that point.

You know what you need to do each day so you can reach your goal. You need to plan your day so your cold calls can be done in the time chunks that were designated for that specific activity. Continue to make time chunks for other tasks like reading and responding to emails.

Scheduling

Someone once said, "If you don't schedule it, it won't get done." You need to block out times on your calendar for any activity that is important in achieving your goals. This is very important if your work environment has other people who can schedule appointments for you. Place alerts on your calendar to remind you of specific activities that you need to do.

Get Rid of Distractions

If you have designated a couple of hours every day to write, you have to keep every distraction at bay. Close all tabs on your internet browser and remove your cell phone from your desk so you won't be tempted to check social media or texts. If you have to, let co-workers, family, and friends know that during this time you are not to be distracted.

Find Common Ground

After you have written down everything you have to do in one week, start looking for what they have in common. Which items are related to career, relationships, or finances?

Chunk these items on your task list that work with the common areas of your life — spirituality, finances, career/work, time, relationships, emotions, and health.

Let's say you are having a problem with your significant other or you forgot your best friend's birthday. You might have a family reunion that you need to cook for, among other things you absolutely have "to do". All of these items can go under the heading of "relationships."

Tweak and Revisit If Needed

You have tried to time chunk for one week and nothing has changed. You might have failed and didn't get as much done as you used to. No need to worry. This is why we practice self-control. This has to be practiced since it isn't something that can be quickly learned.

If you have always been disorganized, then this approach is going to be very hard at first. Try a couple of things and adjust your time chunking, planning, or goals accordingly. Find one thing that works for you and perfect it until you reach the productivity level you are looking for.

The Outcome

After you have chunked all your tasks together, you will be able to see the results you want. In the example above, you want to improve your relationships with friends and loved ones. Once you can see the ultimate purpose, instead of having to check off an endless number of items from a task list, you are going to feel less stress and more productive.

When you can begin to think about your tasks as desired outcomes or clusters, you will be able to keep stress away and learn to focus on larger goals instead of getting overwhelmed by tiny details. Why does this happen? We begin to feel inspired instead of being forced to keep going. When we feel inspired, we come up with a better game plan in order to get there.

There are many things that are demanding our attention. If we don't make conscious efforts to figure out in advance what things we need to focus on, we are going to live with all the demands at that moment. Being able to focus gives us the ultimate power that will change how we feel, how we think, and what we do each moment of our day. Once we are able to change the way we focus, we will be able to change our lives.

Chapter 13:
Reduce Environmental Distractions

Someone asks you what your plans for the weekend are and it might feel like some welcome time off from your busy work week. Time goes by and in 15 minutes, you find out you are late for an important meeting. The stress is back.

It might seem like our places of work were designed to break our focus. Even if you have a bunch of work piling up, you will still take the time to check Twitter, emails, and try to find a cheap flight for vacation even if your manager disapproves. These types of distractions are costly and stressful. It can take around 23 minutes to get your focus back after getting distracted.

The Overload Research Group found that workers in the United States waste around 25 percent of their time trying to deal with incessant streams of data. This loses employers about $997 billion each year.

Let's look at eleven of the most common distractions that we face daily and find ways to deal with them or getting rid of them completely.

1. Personal Technology

Smart watches and smartphones have caused the line between professional and personal communication to become blurred. You now get work calls and emails on the same device along with all kinds of personal information, Instagram photos, and private Facebook comments.

Because of technology's addictive nature, trying to implement policies to control them being used during work hours isn't always effective. It is just as hard to enforce rules about what workers can view on their personal devices.

It is better if people can understand and manage these challenges by themselves. You and your co-workers might agree to put away your phones for a specific time throughout the day. This will help you focus on your work.

2. Email

Most of the email we receive every day are not important. We have the need to look at them as soon as we get them. Here are some ways to manage these messages so they don't mess up your important tasks.

Schedule specific times to check: Turn off your notification alert for emails. Only check and respond to emails at a specified time every day. Give yourself no more than 30 minutes for every set time. Manage your customer's, manager's, and co-worker's expectations about when and how you are going to reply to them.

Pick times of low productivity: There will be a specific time during your day when you are at your best. This could be during the mornings or after lunch. Schedule a time to check email during your less productive times and save your peak energy time for work that is very important.

Turn email into actions: If it takes you longer than a couple of minutes to read and reply to emails, add them to a task list.

Use the trash icon: You don't need to keep email forever. When you do, you could lose sight of the important ones when your inbox gets too full. Your inbox will be harder to manage. After you have replied to them, delete the ones you don't need. Place the ones you want to keep in a separate folder.

Sync smartphones: Try to redirect your email to your smartphones. This will help you keep your computers free of distraction. Apply the above device to your own personal devices.

3. Social Media

Social media gives us ways to communicate with a huge number of people. It could also kill productivity, breaks our concentration, and takes our attention from tasks that need to be done.

Businesses can't block a person's access to websites that aren't work-related. Smartphones get us around all that since they operate on cell towers that don't rely on work-based internet access. People have to be encouraged to responsibly use social media so their focus and productivity don't get affected.

Try to track your social media activity for one week and jot down the time you spend on these sites while working. Schedule some time every day to answer messages or post updates.

4. Instant Messaging

Most workplaces use an Instant Messenger to keep co-workers in touch with each other. It could also be a distraction thanks to emojis and notifications that aren't important. Make a habit of using instant messenger to make fast, small inquiries and not for long conversations. Don't be pressured to reply instantly and set certain times throughout the day to be online.

5. Browsing

Ordering things online, checking the latest sports scores, and reading the latest headlines could easily take 30 minutes out of your time. It could also be breaking workplace rules. Turning off the internet isn't an option since organizations are using software that is cloud-based that takes internet connections to work. You could install software that blocks certain websites or any content you don't want to see. If your workplace agrees to it, use a brief personal browsing session to reward yourself for two hours of quality work.

6. Phone Calls

When a phone rings, it prompts an urgent need to answer it even if you were in deep thought. In order to minimize this distraction, try to arrange a rotation so co-workers could take the calls of another co-worker. They could use instant messenger to check to see if the person could take the call. If you can't turn off your phone due to family concerns, try to preprogram some fast text replies like — "I'm in a meeting, will return your call as soon as possible." You might try to explain to family and friends that you can only receive a call during the evenings or at lunch.

7. Work Environment

Instead of ignoring these distractions like loud co-workers or smelling your favorite food cooking, move away from the distraction. Put yourself in an empty room to gain your focus. Wear headphones that cancel out all noises or play white noise in the background. Whatever it takes to get your attention back.

8. Confusion

Try to have a task list that is manageable. If it is too long, it will lead to procrastination as you try to figure out what to do next. Commit to doing the two most important tasks today and save the rest for tomorrow.

If you find that you are constantly dealing with unplanned and urgent inquiries, go deeper and use techniques to uncover their cause. When you address these problems, you can minimize the disruption or possibly eliminate it completely. You are part of a team. Ask co-workers to help with the load when times get busy. If you are the manager, learn to delegate.

9. People

If your team isn't a virtual one, co-workers might visit your desk and distract you. If you are a manager, you want to be available to your team members. When you are focusing on a task and don't want to be disturbed, try working from home or in an unused room to avoid interruptions. If you have an office, close your door and let your workers know you can't be disturbed for a specific amount of time.

- If your office has an open floor plan, remove chairs or stand up when a co-worker arrives to make your space not as hospitable.

- If you have a certain person who always disturbs you, talk to them about it. They might not realize they are bothering you.

10. You

You need a lot of physical and mental energy in order to juggle priorities, have discipline to control the use of technology, and manage visitors. It is very important that you take time to care for yourself.

Most people don't sleep enough due to the distraction of technology in the home. You need to do your best there as well.

Dehydration makes you feel tired and could impact the way you think. You need to drink a lot of water. Get out in nature. Take a walk around the neighborhood. Don't eat snacks with lots of sugar or heavy lunches. This could lead to little or no concentration later on in your day. Researchers have found that you could improve your time management and performance by realizing that some distractions are going to happen and be prepared for them.

11. Environmental Distractions

If we aren't invested in our work, we act like crows. This means we try to find all the shiny objects around us to distract us from working. Try to declutter your work and home. Get rid of trash and anything that is a distraction and not practical to your task at hand.

Have two work areas if at all possible. What you use daily should be put in the primary area. Things you use either weekly or monthly can go into the secondary area. Things like staplers, photos, printers, cables, books, etc.

Each object needs to have a place of its own. When you have finished using a particular item, return it back to where it needs to be. This keeps everything organized and you will be able to find every item when needed.

In Summary

All of us face distraction each day. It lowers productivity and increases our stress. Figure out what causes you the most distractions during your workday. You might find technology will be at the top of the list.

Try to create new habits to control these distractions. Be careful with your phone, email usage, social media usage, and messaging usage. Let people know that you don't want to be disturbed. Move away from environments that distract you and find a quiet place to work. Keep your task list manageable and concise. If you can implement these things, it might mean you and your co-workers will get more work done.

Stephen Patterson

Chapter 14:
Avoid Being Bored

Boredom isn't caused by not having enough things to do. It isn't even caused by not having things you would like to do. Boredom is often mislabeled to hid different problems. This is the reason why many attempts to stop being bored won't work. They aren't addressing the main problem. Here are some tricks to find the actual culprit behind being bored.

Find out what you actually want to do. Boredom will sometimes mask a problem when you want to do something but another thing is keeping you from it. This might happen when you would like to watch a particular show but your cable is out. If this happens, your first step to kill the boredom is to recognize what activity you want to do.

Get your compass straight. Boredom could be caused by not having a certain direction. Take some time to identify your passions, desires, or goals. At times just thinking about these could get you motivated.

Socialize. Get out of the house and meet up with friends or even make new ones. Boredom might be disguising a need for social energy. Even if you don't know how to meet new people or your friends have other obligations, find an online forum that shares your interests or call a friend.

Learn new things. You might just need some mental stimulation. Here are some things you can do to begin learning new things.

- Write a story
- Research something you are interested in
- Read a book
- Practice your artistic skills

Get rid of distractions. Boredom can be created if you are doing tasks that don't mean anything such as watching a show that isn't holding your interest or randomly surfing the internet. Turn off the computer or television and move around until you figure out something better to do.

Fill up your schedule. Having too much time is just as bad as having no time. It is hard to adjust to boredom when you suddenly have time on your hands. You might find you get irritated during the holidays when your schedule suddenly becomes empty. Take some time to fill in an empty schedule to keep boredom at bay.

Be your own cheerleader. You might be bored because you don't have any confidence. You don't want to work on goals if you have been told you won't succeed. Take time to look at your successes so you can get your confidence back and keep going forward.

Meditate. This is a great activity when you have an extreme case of boredom. Check out online sites about how to do it and why it is good for you.

Journal. Start a word document and just begin writing. This is similar to meditation but a bit more active and not as imaginative.

Find a new challenge. If you realize you are constantly bored, this means you have some time where you don't have anything that will meet your needs. Find a new hobby, challenge, or goal to take up that time.

These are only a few methods that could help you combat boredom. These are only suggestions. The best way to get rid of boredom is to understand why you are bored. Boredom usually has one of five root causes. Figure out that cause and you will be closer to finding a cure.

Procrastination: You aren't really bored. You are procrastinating. Find out what tasks you aren't doing and get rid of procrastination.

Lack of Energy: Being bored isn't the same thing as exhaustion. It can happen when you have more of one type of energy but are exhausted in useful energy. This happens when you find yourself not wanting to work but you don't feel tired physically. Figure out an activity that will use the overabundance of energy. This might mean you have to do physical things after you have spent your day writing. You may also need to be creative after you have spent the day writing boring codes.

Schedule Gaps: You've had a sudden change in your schedule and you don't have a bunch of activities to keep you busy. The answer is to add more tasks. At times you might need to settle into the quiet and use the time to reflect.

Environmental Obstacles: Being away from the internet, being on a long plane ride, and standing in line. These examples of boredom force you to become creative until the situation can be changed.

Cure for the Procrastination Puzzle

No motivation: You don't have any motivation to do what you need to in order to get rid of boredom. For short periods of time, this can be fixed by using some simple tricks. For longer periods of time, you have to address this with some reflection time, reestablish your priorities, and setting some goals.

The first list is suggestions to help you overcome boredom or you could figure out your own after you have found the root of the problem.

Stephen Patterson

Chapter 15:
Find an Accountability Partner

When you are making goals and trying to achieve them, you shouldn't overlook how important an accountability partner can be. You could always accomplish more when somebody is beside you supporting, motivating, and encouraging you every step of the way.

Importance
You need to think about your accountability partner as a mastermind group. They need to have four pillars — motivating, positive, non-competitive, and intimate.

When you are looking for the right partner, you need to find somebody that has a giving presence and not someone who only thinks about themselves. If you see a partner that helps others without asking for anything in return, they are demonstrating the non-competitive and positive pillars. What you might not know is if they are cultivating a relationship of sharing details about your blog or your business plan.

Try to select the correct personality. Trust is only earned with time. Test the waters before you spill all of your beans. You need to find the right person who believes you are able to achieve your goals in spite of your current problems. This is needed to have success.

Why A Partner Is Important

An accountability partner will strengthen your why. If you don't know your "why", you need to find it. This will allow you to understand what your goals will look like and keep you on task and help you achieve your goals.

After you know your why, share it with your accountability partner. This will help them understand the reason why you do what you do. They will be able to relate better to you and will be able to remind you about your why when you forget. You might be making the wrong choices and thinking about other people's why instead of yours.

They will show off your strengths. If you have taken time to find the right partner, you will realize that they will be able to see your strengths and encourage you.

They could help you by having you add stuff to your page or even find new areas for you to branch out to help your income.

They can see your weaknesses. It won't take long to find somebody's weaknesses. If your accountability partner is perfect, you will feel secure in your relationship. This means when your partner shows you a weakness that is holding you back, you have to understand that they aren't attacking you personally but are trying to help you improve.

When someone shows a weakness, they need to suggest a solution too. This is done to encourage more learning by attending a conference, taking a class, or reading a book.

Accountability partners need to be sounding boards. They are great to bounce ideas off of. This can only be achieved if you trust each other and they have proven their loyalty.

In this world, everyone has things they need to vent about. If you have a blog, try to keep these short and stay away from getting into a long, negative discussion. The purpose of a blog is for growth and positivity.

- You need to look for solutions for problems you are venting about or vent to your spouse.

- Always take the time to celebrate goals and milestones you have reached because these reflect what is necessary and important.

- They will help you set goals. Accountability partners can keep you motivated by setting goals.

After you have decided on your goals and have taken the steps of making goals you need to reach each month, you can hold somebody accountable while they are holding you accountable. Create a social media group that will help you make sure you are keeping up with the daily tasks that will get you to your goals.

They will learn with you. You will learn to love it when your accountability partner is attending the same conference, taking the same classes, or reading the same book. It makes it easy to talk about how to put in into your own success. Figuring out if things are or aren't working is another way to learn together.

They make great mastermind groups. After you know the how, why, when, what, and who of your group would consist of and their guidelines, you can place the four pillars and begin growing together.

Chapter 16:
Leverage Your Peak-Energy

Hours are not created equal. At times, one hour is enough time to get through a large project. Other times, one hour only allows you to some of a few emails.

CEOs, performance coaches, and motivational speakers urge you to find and leverage your peak hours as a way to be more productive. If you can learn to follow a schedule that utilizes the work hours when you are more productive, this makes sure your projects get the energy they deserve. Here is a plan to help you harness your power hours.

Ultradian Rhythm
Humans run on cycles like everything else in nature. There is growing research about ultradian rhythms. These are cycles that last about 90 to 120 minutes that run in our bodies a 24-hour circadian day. This suggests that each day is driven by cycles that can change how productive and alert we are.

When the cycle starts, we will have more focus and energy. Toward the end, we might begin feeling fatigued and scatterbrained. If your computer is lagging from all those tabs you have opened, you are running in an energy valley.

Having a title of "workaholic" may sound great but that fact of the matter is productivity will drop when you have worked 50 hours or more in only one week. When talking about output, working during your best hours might be better than working longer hours. This is great news.

You need to work during your peak hours when you are feeling excited and alert, especially if your project involves critical decisions, complex thoughts, and problem-solving.

If you try to do these projects when you are in your energy valley, you are going to have to fight with your foggy brain and the project is going to take a lot longer and it will be more painful.

Less complex, unimportant, and routine tasks are easily done when you aren't engaged or focused. When you are feeling sleepy, you could still sit through a weekly meeting. You might have to prop your eyelids open, but who doesn't.

When you know what to do when you have your next surge of energy, you can be assured you will be able to achieve your goals on any given day.

People who are self-employed get to choose the hours they work. There are many companies that now offer work from home options and flexible hours to their employees. There are millions of professionals who have the opportunity to work when they feel productive, inspired, and alert.

All of this sounds great, but it takes us to this question — how can you know when you are at your most productive?

How Introversion and Extraversion Leverage Your Energy
You might be wondering what extraversion and introversion are all about. What is more important is how it could help you. Here are a few tips on getting to the root of these buzzwords and some advice on how to leverage your type.

Let's get rid of the misconception that introverts are wallflowers and extraverts are social butterflies. The Swiss psychiatrist, Carl Jung, created these terms. He defined them this way, "The key to finding your style and creating your optimal flow – is understanding where you gain the most energy."

Introverts get energy from their inner selves. This is where their memories, emotions, and ideas live. They feel alive when they research, think, write, and read. Around one-third of the world's workforce is introverted. The funny thing is they might not look like they are.

Extroverts get energy from the outside world. This comes from activities, experiences, and people. They feel alive when they are taking action and engaging externally.

The bottom line is extraversion and introversion are about the energy you get from the stimulation in either your outer or inner world.

Self-Assessment

You are probably wondering, "I like to spend time in both worlds. How can I know which one I like better?" The truth is, we all go between the outer and inner world every day.

The key is to find your true style and create your optimal flow. Basically, you need to understand where you get the most energy.

If you still aren't sure, think about doing activities that will either drain or energize you for a whole week. You might find a pattern that specific people or responsibilities are very draining. That is good information to know.

To quote Susan Cain, "The key to maximizing our talents is for us all to put ourselves in a zone of stimulation that is right for us."

Find activities that take you from baseline energy to being purely invigorated. See if they are in your outer or inner world. Commit to watching for the entire period and you might find more energy and focus in one of them over the other.

Now that you can see where you are getting your energy from, leverage it.

Introverts: Support Your Inner World

Time to Reflect: If your boss wants you to brainstorm ideas right now or another asks for feedback, you need to allow yourself some space to reflect by telling them you will get back to them after you have had some time to reflect of their problems.

Find Private Times and Space: Wear headphones that cancel out noises. Find time at night for yourself. Find a room that nobody uses at work. Take time for some one-on-one time with a significant other at home. Give yourself the time you need to get into your inner world without being interrupted.

Choose to Communicate in Writing: It is totally fine if meetings aren't your way of getting your thoughts across. Capture your energy and clarity from that inner world by writing email or memos. Writing becomes your support tool when you need to get your thoughts across to others.

Extraverts: Make Opportunities in Your Outer World

Have Conversation Offline: If email exchanges with co-workers feel like they are endless, take the time to talk with them in person or pick up the phone. The answer might come to you in a quick chat or by going on a coffee run. You will get energized with the interaction.

Work Out Ideas by Talking: Find a confidant that helps you generate ideas. They are also great to bounce ideas off of. You will go further by this approach.

Place Yourself Where You Can Engage with Others: If you have to work on the weekend, try working at a coffee shop instead of an empty office. Get off that treadmill and find a running partner. Create opportunities that put you in environments that will stimulate you more.

Knowing what your energy and communication style is doesn't mean you put yourself in a box. Many people realize they either belong at one end or the other of the spectrum. With time, you will be able to develop a comfortable place so you can step out of your character mode. It doesn't matter if you think you are an extrovert or an introvert, you have to actively identify and find situations that will play to you.

Stephen Patterson

Chapter 17:
Parkinson's Law

In 1955, famous British author and historian, Cyril Northcote Parkinson said, "Work expands to fill the time available for its completion." This is known as Parkinson's Law. This quote first appeared in the opening line of an article for The Economist. It later became the focus of the book Parkinson's Law: The Pursuit of Progress.

Mr. Parkinson had the qualifications to make this statement because he had worked for the British Civil Service. He had the first-hand experience seeing how bureaucracy works. Bureaucracy is a product of culture because of the limiting belief that we have to work harder is better than being able to work faster and smarter.

The quote "Work expands to fill the time available for its completion". This means if you put a time limit on completing a task in one week that would normally only take you two hours, then this task will get more daunting and complex as the week goes by. You might not even have more work to fill the time frame, but just the tension and stress about knowing you have to get it done causes anxiety. When you assign the correct time for a certain task, you will get more time back and the task won't be as complicated.

Some people think that Parkinson's Law meant that we can give a time limit of one minute to any task and that task will become so simple that we can do it in that one minute. The problem with that is that Parkinson's Law is only an observation and not magic. It works because people will give tasks a time limit of longer than is actually needed. They like having a buffer zone. They don't actually know how long it will take to complete the task. They don't realize how fast certain tasks could be completed until this principle gets tested.

Many employees will defy the rule of "work harder, not smarter". They know that in spite of the better return on investment isn't always appreciated. This is related to the idea that if something takes you longer to complete, the better quality it will be. The rising trend of telecommuting employees is changing for those people who have adapted to this already. Employers don't know what you really are doing with the extra spare time.

Let's see how we can apply Parkinson's Law to everyday life. This will allow you to check off your to-do list faster and won't be spending time trying to fill in time to look busy. This holds true whether or not you work from home or in an office because "work harder, not smarter" is an idea that many people fall into even if their work isn't supervised.

Run Against the Clock

Create your task list and divide it up by how much time is needed to finish each task. Now you are going to give yourself half of that time to finish the tasks. You have to understand this time limit is critical. It must be treated just like all other deadlines. The only way to reverse what we have been taught about "work harder, not smarter" is seeing the deadlines we've set are unbreakable. These are just like the deadlines your clients or boss has set.

You have to use that need for competition to fuel you just like it does with gaming and sports in order for this to work for you. You have to beat the clock. Beat it just like it was an actual real-life opponent. Don't take shortcuts or produce any low-quality output. This helps if you don't take your own deadlines to heart.

This is going to begin as an exercise to see if you are accurate when figuring out your time projections for your tasks. Some might be spot on and some might be too long. The ones you predicted as spot on might not get met because when you half the time, you actually didn't have enough time. You need to experiment with longer times. Don't go right back to the original time since there might be a better time in between the two.

If you work from a computer, its timer will be useful when you begin this. It will save you some time because the timer lets you see how much more time you have. Using a clock does take some simple math.

Kill the Cockroaches in The World of Productivity

Find these time fillers such as feed reading and emails that might take you 10, 20, or even 30 minutes. In the productivity world, these are called cockroaches. These pests that don't do anything but make life a pain in the rear. You can't get rid of these pains no matter what you try or how much you try.

Don't allow yourself 20 to 30 minutes to check emails. Instead, give yourself five minutes. If you like challenges, give yourself only two minutes. Don't go back to these tasks until you have completed everything on your task list for the day. After all the tasks have been done, then you can indulge in reading all your emails, checking social media, and feed reading all you want. Spending all your spare time doing these things isn't recommended.

Only about ten percent of these tasks are important. The other 90 percent are totally useless. This makes you focus on the tasks that are important. Just experiment on how much you can actually do in less time. Figure out what makes an email important. Enforce some strict guidelines and create harsh penalties if you slip up. This means using your delete button more.

Experiment with Parkinson's Law and see how far down you can squash your deadlines in all areas of your life. Be aware of the fine line between not enough time and bare minimum. You need to do a job well done in a little amount of time. You don't want to create a disaster that might lose you your job or clients.

Stephen Patterson

Chapter 18:
Prioritize Tasks

You have so much work to do at this moment. Your list is a mess of items and you don't have any idea on how to prioritize them. There are some ways to get your list prioritized without any effort. You can actually apply any of these in just five minutes and know what you need to do next. There have been various methods over the years, with each having their own considerations and quirks.

How do you know what is right for you? Let's look at four ways to help you prioritize your tasks.

Put Your Tasks into Four Boxes: Important Vs. Urgent

This prioritization method comes from former President Dwight D Eisenhower. In the year 1954, he was quoted as saying, "I have two kinds of problems: the urgent and the important. The urgent are not important, and the important are never urgent." This quote caused the Eisenhower Matrix to be created. This is a four-box system to organize your tasks by importance and urgency and then doing them.

- The first box will get labeled "Urgent and Important". These are the things you need to do now.

- The second box gets labeled "Important, not urgent." With these tasks, you get to decide when you want to do them.

- The third box gets labeled "Urgent, not important". These tasks get delegated to someone else to do.

- The fourth box gets labeled "Not important and not urgent." These tasks get deleted from your to-do list.

- This Eisenhower Matrix places tasks into two categories and then prioritizes them. It is a quick and easy way to get tasks in order at the beginning of your day.

Action: You need to create a habit of categorizing your tasks quickly by using a checklist like the one below.

The "Important" Tasks:
- Does it require little effort but gives great results?

- You have to finish this task before others will get done.

- It provides value.

- If you don't complete it, it will affect other projects and people.

The "Urgent" Tasks:
- If you don't do it, there will be immediate consequences.
- It needs to be done soon.
- You need to give it immediate attention.
- This task is way overdue.

In order to implement the matrix to your lists, use more tags to figure out which box the task will fall into. Once you check this against your task list, you will easily see what is or isn't a priority.

When Eating Two Frogs, Eat the Ugliest First

This is slightly different from the Eisenhower Matrix. This method of eating frogs looks at your feelings about the tasks on your list.

To quote Mark Twain, "If you eat a live frog each day for breakfast, nothing worse can happen for the rest of the day." The idea is to consume the ugliest frog as early as you can, then the rest of the day will be a breeze. How do you replace frogs with tasks? You put your tasks into four boxes:

- Tasks you hate doing but don't really need to be done.

- Tasks you hate doing but they really need to be done.

- Tasks you like doing and they really need to be done.

- Tasks you like doing but don't really need to be done.

The logic behind this is if you don't like doing the task, it is because it is hard to do. You realize it is important but you just procrastinate. Find the largest, ugliest task done as quickly as possible and the rest will be easy. You can use the tagging method from above for each number to make it even easier.

For Precise Prioritization, Use the ABCDE Method

This method is a bit more mathematical. It shows that various tasks could have the same priority level. You don't randomly do tasks that have the same priority level as you go down your list. This method creates two different levels of priority. Here is how you prioritize your tasks using this method.

- Go through your to-do list and give each task a letter from A to E. A represents the most priority.

- Now, for all the tasks that were given an A, add a number that dictates the order you are going to do them in.

- Continue this until every task has a letter and number.

In order to be sure, you are categorizing them strictly, you have to be hard on yourself. You can't start a new letter until the previous one has been completely done.

If you compare this to the other methods we've already talked about, the A tasks will be the important and urgent frogs.

Choose the One to Three Most Important

This is the simplest way to get your tasks prioritized. Leo Babura states, "At the beginning of each day, review your list and write down one to three MITs or Most Important Tasks that you'd like to accomplish for the day. That's your whole planning system. You don't need any more than that." This quote is from the book Zen to Done.

If you use the other methods above, you should be able to choose your three most important tasks fairly quickly and be on the path to getting your task list down to zero.

This method totally relies on your very own intuition. Once you have done several projects or get swamped by a HUGE task list enough times, you are just going to instinctively know what tasks are going to be the most important.

At the end of the day, there isn't a true mathematical formula to figure it all out, but there are ways to help you prioritize your tasks and making it a habit. This is a skill you can work on to get things done faster.

Chapter 19:
Reward Yourself

You have to set goals and then reward yourself in order to keep yourself motivated to help you succeed. People need to set goals. Yearly, monthly, weekly, daily, and ongoing goals that influence you each day. Some of these goals will be easy. Taking out the trash? Got it. Need to do the dishes? They are done. Some goals can be quite hard to accomplish like trying to have a healthier lifestyle. Why? The main reason the long-term goals are harder is that we can't see any immediate results. You could diet and exercise for months without seeing any changes to your body and it gets discouraging. You need to set goals differently. You need to set goals that come along with rewards.

The Idea Behind Goals and Rewards
You basically need to set measurable and specific goals that will determine a positive reward when you hit that goal. Here is the main part. You need to keep these promises and reward yourself. The goals need to be challenging and attainable. You need to push yourself to do

better at whatever it is you are doing. Let's say you want to give up drinking soda. You have to set a goal of not drinking soda for two weeks in a row. Your reward is to add money to your new wardrobe fund. The better you do, the more money you will have for shopping. Simple!

Before You Begin
You might have to get a bit more formal with yourself to make sure you stay serious when setting goals and rewards. Think about creating a contract. Your contract might read:

"I, (your name here), know that I am trying to improve myself every day. I commit myself to these goals, and in turn, commit to rewarding myself appropriately when a goal has been accomplished. These rewards will be fulfilled without restraint or guilt. I, (your name here), commit myself to this self-care for the duration of this contract, a period of six months."

Then you will sign and date the contract. This will add gravity to set the goal. After you have finished this, you will understand the feeling. It will feel powerful and real when you have it written and signed. This should be done before you head into the fundamentals of rewards and goals. This will make you take the process seriously and this is what you want.

Set the Goal

Your next step will be figuring out what goals you are going to set. You probably already know some aspects of your life you would like to improve. You need to figure out the specifics. You can't set goals that are vague. You need to be specific so you are able to figure out your answer when asked, "Did you reach your goal?"

Setting goals are tricky but can be done. You need to know how to set goals that are challenging but within your reach and that is hard to do. When you do it, it could change your progress. Getting great goals could be the difference between exhilaration and frustration.

To begin, sit down and figure out all the goals you want to set for yourself. Be more creative, drink more water, and exercise more, then think about how you will get to this goal. Try to think about something that if you really tried, you know you can do it even if it is a bit hard. You might want to be more creative, do this task for about 75 percent of the month and the rest you get to do whatever. Track your progress so you can see if you were successful at the end of the month.

Setting Rewards

Once you have all your goals figured out, begin picking out a reward to go along with each goal. This is a bit tricky. You will want to find something that will lure you to work without hurting the goal. The easiest reward is a treat. Candy isn't a reward especially if your goal is health-oriented since it goes against the entire goal. Try to select something such as adding money to your new wardrobe fund or buy yourself a non-food treat. If your goal is related to creativity, try to find a reward that is also related to creativity that encourages you to continue to practice.

Find Balance

You might realize that you are playing a dangerous game. It is easy to be self-indulgent and give yourself a huge reward for a task that was too easy. You might decide you deserve a caramel macchiato from that specialty coffee shop on the corner you pass up each day for each week you go without drinking soda. Just one and no more. You don't want to undermine trying to drink less junk. You need to implement some checks and balances. You may need to bring in a third party.

Before you put in ink your final rewards, have it run by your third party. They will be tough and they won't allow you to get ridiculous.

They might tell you to tone down the reward or set your goals higher. Having someone you can talk this through with will help you see a different side of you. Having another opinion will work wonders, especially if you can't think of any rewards.

If you don't want your rewards to be money related, that is fine. You could just use time. Give yourself a reward of binge playing your favorite video game. You might not have had time to play your game because you've been so busy. If you have a loving partner, ask them if they would be willing to be a reward. They might be willing to give you a foot or back rub. They might be willing to take over a chore or two like doing the dishes or cooking a meal if you meet your goal. You should be able to find rewards that aren't going to break the bank but still be great motivators. You don't always have to have a financial goal. Find something that is fun and enjoyable.

How to Feel Motivated?

You will feel more energized to hit your goals when you know there will be a reward waiting for you. You probably work better if there is a threat of lower income, disapproval of a parent, or a bad grade. Because you don't have anyone watching over you, you have to find ways to motivate yourself.

You will find many times that you might be willing to give up on daily goals and then change your mind because you remembered your reward. That treat might illuminate that light ahead on rough days. Don't forget to show yourself some love and set those goals and rewards. You will be able to accomplish your goals if you just keep the right attitude. The main attitude you need in order to succeed is to tell yourself that "You deserve good things." You absolutely do deserve good things, everyone does. You just need to get out there and grab them.

Chapter 20: FAQs

1. What Does It Mean If More Than One Type of Procrastination Relates to Me?

There is no reason to panic. They are all human traits and it is normal for anyone to be able to identify with all of them. There may be one or two that might jump out at you. The six types represent the outer opinions of three traits:

Attention to Details: A perfectionist will pay too much attention to little details. A dreamer won't give it enough attention.

Focused on the Future: A person who worries is overly concerned about what could happen if…. A person who creates crises isn't concerned enough until it is down to the wire.

Relating to Others: A person who likes to defy will always go against what other people want. A person who pleases understands what other people want.

2. Why Is It So Difficult to Change Procrastination?

Procrastination gets driven by tenacious personality traits and strong emotions. Therefore, it makes it hard to change. If it was simple like making New Year's resolutions or by just doing it, your teacher's scolding and mother's nagging would have cured it many years ago.

In order to change a habit, you have to put into place certain strategies and skills that work with your personal style. This is necessary since advice for one type would be completely wrong for a different one.

3. Everyone Procrastinates, Don't They?

Nobody is perfect. Procrastination will happen. Your closet continues to be messy even after you promised yourself you would clean it. Holding a tough conversation gets delayed until you have no other choice. The response to a certain request will go unanswered.

For many people, procrastination isn't a thing that happens every now and then. It is a deeply rooted, pervasive, and chronic pattern. If you are like this, you know you tend to allow things to slide. Not just the hard tasks but with the easy ones.

4. What Is Procrastination?

We are all the time veering around procrastination. So, what does it mean? Some think it is just laziness. This is so not true. The truth of the matter is procrastination is an approach/avoidance conflict that was never resolved.

There is a part of you that knows you need to do a specific task but other parts will keep you from doing it. You are constantly torn between two conflicts. To quote Hamlet, "To do or not to do." I know that it isn't the right quote but it gets the point across. Being indecisive makes it hard for you to be able to choose a commitment to action.

5. Why Does the Digital Age Make It Harder to Beat Procrastination?

Addictive, appealing, and accessible distractions are everywhere you turn. Social media seduces. Digital devices deter. Entertainment always entices. Diversions are around every corner. Cell phones constantly chatter. If you take the time to add up the time you spend on all the things that don't have anything to do with your career or personal goals, does it really shock you that you are teetering on the edge?

6. What Do I Do If I Know Someone Who Could Really Use Some Help with Their Procrastination?

Get proactive. Purchase this book and give it to them as a gift. You are probably as frustrated watching them as they feel. It is hard watching your family and friends not doing as well as you know they can. Tell them you hope this gift will help them achieve the success they deserve. Now take a step back. You can't do it for them. You can only provide them with the resources they need in order for it to happen.

Conclusion:

Thank you for making it through to the end of Cure Procrastination and Become Productive. Let's hope it was informative and able to provide you with all of the tools you need to achieve your goals whatever they may be.

Procrastination will get you nowhere. You will end up feeling stressed, anxious, angry, and any other negative emotion you can think of. Quit this evil cycle today. Use what you have learned in this book to turn your life around for the better.

If you find this book helpful in anyway a review to support my endeavors is much appreciated.

Stephen Patterson

Cure for the Procrastination Puzzle

www.ingramcontent.com/pod-product-compliance
Lightning Source LLC
Chambersburg PA
CBHW020418080526
44584CB00014B/1394